70 Stories
about
Boston University

1 9 2 3 – 1 9 9 3

To Martha

cordially

— Dean George

70 Stories
about
Boston University

1 9 2 3 – 1 9 9 3

A Memoir

by

George K. Makechnie

BOSTON UNIVERSITY

Boston University, Boston 02215
© 1993 by the Trustees of Boston University
All rights reserved. Published 1993
Printed in the United States of America

*Photographs (except p. 21 cen.) courtesy of Boston
University Office of Photo Serivces; p. 21 cen. courtesy of
Ralph Norman Studios, Boston.*

On the cover: Drawing of idealized campus from a
building fund prospectus, "Boston University — Its
Goal," 1923/24; courtesy of Boston University Special
Collections.

Library of Congress Cataloging-in-Publication Data

Makechnie, George K. (George Kinsley), 1907–
    70 stories about Boston University 1923–1993 : a memoir / by George K. Makechnie.
        p.   cm.
    ISBN 0-87270-104-2
    1. Boston University — History — 20th century. 2. Makechnie, George K. (George
Kinsley), 1907 — Biography. I. Title. II. Title: Seventy stories about Boston University
1923–1993.
LD513.M35 1993
378.744'61 — dc20   93-4005
                                                                        CIP

Contents

Preface / *vii*

Acknowledgments / *ix*

Introduction *by Trudi Smith* / *xi*

O N E
The Daniel L. Marsh Era / 1

T W O
The Harold C. Case Era / 57

T H R E E
The Arland F. Christ-Janer Years / 95

F O U R
The John Silber Era / 111

F I V E
Reflections / 147

Dean George nails a sign on the door of Sargent College in Cambridge announcing the move to the Charles River Campus. 1958.

Preface

M Y ASSOCIATION with Boston University began seventy years ago — "The years of our life." It was my widowed mother who, in spite of strained financial circumstances, insisted that I take the college preparatory course in high school. I had opted for the commercial course in the belief that it was the shortest route to a badly needed family income. But she said, "We will find a way to raise college tuition money." That way came when I got a job as groundsman at Sears Chapel in Longwood. It was she who made sure that I appreciated every blessing and was guided by a sense of service that Marian Wright Edelman describes so tellingly today: "Service to others is the rent we pay for the privilege of living." In 1923, Michael O'Niel, submaster of Everett High School, where I was a junior, counseled with me about post-secondary school education. Knowing of my circumstances, that financial restraints and the needs of a widowed mother required that I be within commuting distance, he talked to me about Boston University. I recall that he said, "Boston University isn't much for campus and buildings, but its academic offering is of high quality." He mentioned Warren Ault and Edgar Brightman as tops in their respective fields of history and philosophy. He, himself, had studied at Boston University. I visited the University and found O'Niel's assessment valid; the College of Business Administration building on Boylston Street reeked of old age, and not one blade of grass relieved its austere environment. But the faculty: "tops." The University's bulletin noted that Lemuel Murlin was president.

As assistant to Dean Arthur Wilde of the School of Education, in 1932, I would be privileged to meet Murlin at the University Commencement, at which he received an honorary degree. Later I would learn that it was he who sensed the peril of University expenditures exceeding income and who insisted that the budget be balanced annually. I also learned that in Murlin's administration the land today known as the "Charles River Campus" was purchased and that he drew up the original plan for the development of the campus. His successor, Daniel L. Marsh, with some modifications, implemented the plan.

The seventy stories in this little book are about events that I personally experienced. Only a few sentences of "connective tissue" are employed to give a semblance of continuity to the work. Except where longitudinal events are involved, the stories fall under the headings of the presidencies of Daniel Marsh, Harold Case, Arland Christ-Janer, and John Silber.

— G.K.M.

Acknowledgments

T HREESCORE AND TEN" are the years of my relationship to Boston University. From an introduction to the University by the submaster of my high school in 1923 to my continuing experience of the dynamism of the institution under the leadership of John Silber in 1993, mine has been a privilege perhaps unique in the annals of Boston University. Welcoming new students in September 1992 brought into focus a realization that their parents were still to be born when I first arrived here in that long-ago time. But each fall, the coming of the new students and the return of upperclassmen continue to be charged with the excitement of new beginnings and of a renewed sense that life is a continuum.

It has been a joy to review these events of bygone days and have them return in sharp relief, and to record experiences in the present exciting scene. To have Trudi Smith as a partner in the effort has been especially rewarding. From the perspective of youth, she has brought her unusual skills as editor and writer to the effort. She has written the introduction. She has performed with a lilt that made the work plain fun!

A thank you to Lisa Libbares, whose skills with the gadgets of modernity — word processors, spelling checks, computer discs, and the like — made for a speedy transition from my handwritten pages to a neatly typed manuscript. Ah yes, and for graciousness and patience with me for those successions of "last" readings which made for changes of a word or phrase.

A word of appreciation to Natalie McCracken, who gave encouragement along the way and after the last of the "last readings" of the manuscript did the final editorial scrutiny.

Thank you, Sam McCracken, for first suggesting that I record these stories.

Dean George walks briskly over the Boston University Bridge in the year of his retirement. 1972.

INTRODUCTION

by Trudi Smith

W HEN GEORGE KINSLEY MAKECHNIE takes a walk, anyone who joins him is in for a workout. At eighty-six, Makechnie prefers to walk as he always has: briskly. His gait, like his manner, is steady, direct, and unflagging. It is an eloquent testimony to a lifetime dedicated to fitness, not only of body, but also of mind and spirit.

He was born in Everett, Massachusetts, to a family whose arrival in New England predated the Revolutionary War. Dr. John McKechnie, a Scot, was the forefather who settled in Winslow, Maine. Among his occupations was medicine; he was a physician who once tended to Colonel Benedict Arnold and his troops. By the mid-1800s, members of the McKechnie clan were settling in Boston. Hiram McKechnie, a clothier, opened a shop in 1856. At the urging of his partner, Myron Wilmot, who feared "McKechnie" would be taken for Irish, he adopted an "Americanized" spelling — Makechnie. Although the store remained open for only three years, the spelling stuck and, from then on, was taken by all family members who moved to Boston.

George W. Makechnie, Hiram's brother and the great-grandson of Dr. John McKechnie, came to Boston in 1871. He married Sarah Ann Cram shortly thereafter, and the two settled in Everett. George, who owned a men's clothing store, was known for his benevolence. When he knew a customer was having a hard time, he would wrap extra clothes in with a purchase of a single item. George and Sarah, both devoted Baptists and Republicans, tried to impart their staunch ideology to their five children. Their eldest son, Charles, was never truly indoctrinated, and the rift with his parents grew after he married Mabel Downing. When the young couple formed a dance club for married couples, the elder Makechnies were appalled (to say nothing of their minister's hell-threatening disdain), their religious sensibilities offended. Neither Charles nor Mabel were regular churchgoers either, which only exacerbated the concern the elder Makechnies had for their son, and eventually, for their grandson.

Mabel gave birth to George Kinsley Makechnie on January 6, 1907. Eight months later, Charles contracted typhoid fever from contaminated oysters and died, at the age of thirty-one. Uncomfortable with the hard-line views of her in-laws, Mabel and her young son moved into the home of her father, George Downing, a fourteen-room house at #1 Dean Street in Everett. Soon Mabel joined the International Bible Students' Association, a group that gave Mabel faith that her husband would not languish in Hell but would rise again. Young George was thus surrounded by varying views of religion — from that of his mother's Bible study group to that of his Baptist grandparents to that of his non-churchgoing Catholic grandfather, George Downing. The Baptist Makechnies took their grandson to their church every other Sunday, where often he would hear sermons condemning Catholics as well as his mother's Bible study group. The conflicting beliefs served to confuse young George, causing him to begin early his search for spirituality unencumbered by "self-imposed walls."

Mabel's determination profoundly affected her son. A woman who never remarried and who supported herself and her son by taking in lodgers and stitching tennis balls, she taught George to face life's hardships head-on. When Grandfather Downing died and the open casket lay in the living room, Mabel made sure that her six-year-old son saw the body, telling him, "This you do to strengthen yourself." She encouraged him to stand up for his beliefs; he began adhering to her advice at an early age, parading through Everett Square with the suffragettes, carrying a sign that read "Votes for Women."

Despite their limited financial resources, Mabel decided early on that George must seek higher education. Ninth grade marked the time an academic path had to be chosen. George had already filled out an application for a commercial course, thinking that was the fastest way to begin earning money. Mabel, however, wanted her son to take college preparatory classes, so she took him to meet with Wilbur Jerome Rockwood, principal of the Everett High School, at his summer home in Yarmouth, Nova Scotia. By the time they left, George was convinced to aim for university, although he was still worried about the impending expense. A one-time boarder at #1 Dean Street came through with a job for George as groundskeeper at the Sears Chapel in Longwood. Not only did the position enable George to save money for college, but it helped him realize that wisdom is gleaned not just from educated intellectuals, but also from gardeners, janitors, groundsmen, and cooks. Indeed, throughout his tenure at Boston University, he frequently turned to those who work with their hands for advice and inspiration.

George's decision to apply to Boston University, then a commuter school, was made with the guidance of Everett High School submaster Michael O'Niel. George entered the University in 1925, enrolling in the College of Business Administration — again, he assumed that a practical course would enable him to earn a better income in the long run. Yet George was plagued with the knowledge that business was not his true calling. Vivid memories of teachers, coupled with male role models such as O'Niel, who were also educators, soon led him to a conference with Arthur Wilde, dean of the School of Education. The meeting confirmed what George already knew: he was meant to be an educator, and thus he changed his course of study in the academic year 1926–1927.

Upon George's graduation in 1929, Dean Wilde made him a flattering invitation: to stay on at Boston University, pursue a master's degree, and work for him part-time as his assistant. Despite an offer of a teaching position at the prestigious Bay Path Institute, Wilde was able to convince him that an advanced degree was essential. One notable duty George was called upon to do was to address an assembly at Sargent School in Cambridge, Massachusetts, in 1929. A week later, Dean Wilde showed him a letter from Ledyard Sargent, school owner, offering the Sargent School as a gift to Boston University. These early contacts with the college would soon become the focus of George's University career.

Upon earning his master's in 1931, George was offered the post of full-time assistant to Dean Wilde. He joined the School of Education faculty, teaching history and social sciences there and at Sargent. As the University's liaison to Sargent College, George was faced with other pressing tasks. Immediately after his appointment, he and Dean Wilde set out to locate a suitable site for a camp for Sargent College, as camping was an integral part of the curriculum. After scouring New England, the two came back convinced that the only truly appropriate site was the camp in Peterborough, New Hampshire, that was originally owned by Dr. Dudley Sargent and associates, but was not a part of the gift to Boston University. George was already quite familiar with the camp, having represented the dean there during the summer of 1930. By 1932, the dean had persuaded the corporation that owned the camp to sell and the University (despite the Great Depression) to buy the property. Perhaps part of George's devotion to the camp was purely sentimental: it was there in 1931 that he had first met Anne Schonland, then president of Sargent's Student Council and ultimately the love of his life.

Anne and George were married on June 12, 1933. After a short honeymoon in Maine, the two returned so that George could continue teaching. Through the 1930s and early 1940s, George taught a number of classes at the University. He also taught external courses, primarily for the Harvard–Boston University Extension Program. He often taught classes, particularly in sociology, at nursing schools (such as Peter Bent Brigham Hospital and Boston Children's Hospital) and also gave commencement addresses at such schools *pro bono*. He contributed articles to a number of educational journals, a practice that continued throughout his career. During the 1930s, he progressed from his initial position at the School of Education to registrar, and ultimately, to professor and director of undergraduate studies in 1941. In 1937, George spearheaded a feasibility study for opening a nursing program at Boston University. A division of nursing education was established in the School of Education in 1938. Its success led to the opening of the School of Nursing in 1946. George's advocacy helped establish him as godparent of the school.

Wartime brought a new dimension to George's work; in 1943 he was recruited to direct the curriculum for the Civil Affairs Training School at Boston University. Designed to train senior officers of the

United States Army for allied military government service, the program was implemented at only nine other universities nationwide. Beyond providing essential training for Army officers, the school enabled George to showcase the considerable skills he had acquired as a higher education administrator. His demonstration of effective leadership was perhaps the last hurdle on the ascent to deanship.

In August 1945, President Daniel Marsh named George dean of Sargent College. Although not schooled in physical education (the college's primary curriculum), Dean George (as he became affectionately known by students and others) had proven himself an able administrator. In the first few weeks of deanship, he was given the task of finding suitable housing in Cambridge for a black student because she was not allowed to live in the college dormitories. Dean George, who had once left a professional fraternity over its exclusive "no blacks allowed" policy, found the task abhorrent. He informed the Admissions Office that he would never perform that job again and quietly spread the word that from then on, the Sargent dorms were to be desegregated.

Another area that needed immediate attention was Sargent Camp. Over the years, the underutilized space had fallen into disarray, only open for the Sargent College program in June and September and as a girls' camp in the summer. In the fall of 1946, Dean George approached President Marsh with ideas for a year-round camp that offered the credit-bearing curriculum of outdoor activities for Sargent students and also responded to the demand for school camping programs and recreational weekends for schoolchildren and adults. Expecting a year-long discussion, Dean George was astonished when the president said, "George, I have every confidence in your ability to put that into effect." "When?" he gasped. "Now," was the reply. Thus began Dean George's task as director of Sargent Camp to phase out the summer camp, winterize the buildings, and initiate the various programs.

On Fridays, the Makechnies would pack up their three children — Norman, Arthur, and Joan — the dog, and the dormitory cook, and head to Peterborough. Finally, in 1949, the family moved to Windy Row in Peterborough, and Dean George began his daily commute to Boston. His time directing Sargent Camp made him an expert on camping, and he initiated school camping programs for public and private schools there and throughout New England and in Paris (where he contributed to the formation of the International Association for Physical Education for Girls and Women). Still a contributing writer for several educational publications, he often wrote about camping programs and outdoor education.

Dean George's dream for Sargent College was that it would realize and build on the original wishes of its founder, Dudley Allen Sargent. Sargent's main focus was not on physical education for its recreational value, but for its preventative and healing aspects. Dean George's concept was to take Sargent's visionary attitudes a step further, developing a holistic view of allied health. He envisioned a curriculum that blended elements of a liberal arts education with Sargent's scientific focus. By 1952, with President Case's approval, Dean George was ready to implement the beginnings of what would become the total allied health concept. This brought the Makechnies back to the Boston area; they moved to a Revolutionary War–period house on Massachusetts Avenue in Lexington. Sargent Camp, serving more than one thousand people each year, had earned its first full-time director.

The year 1953 marked a turning point in Dean George's life. President Case had invited Howard Thurman, then head of the Church for the Fellowship of All Peoples, the first fully integrated church in America, to become dean of Marsh Chapel. Sue Bailey Thurman, Howard's wife, remembers the beginnings of what was to become a deep and lasting friendship:

> As to George Makechnie and Howard Thurman, their spirits met before they met in person. It seems intended that George should have written the first letter warmly welcoming Howard to the new, unprecedented post as dean of the chapel at Boston University. Unprecedented because it marked the first time a black man had been called to a "deanship" in any white college or university in America. George's welcoming letter was prophetic of things to come.

Along with sharing a wedding anniversary, the two soon found they had character-shaping elements in common: childhoods marked by the early death of their fathers; strong, committed mothers; and, for each, a prolonged quest to fulfill a spiritual yearning that was not satisfied by organized religion.

Having attended just one of Thurman's services, the Makechnies became devoted congregants. Finally Dean George had found a worship service that excluded no person and broke down the barriers of divisiveness so often erected by organized religions. Thurman preached a love ethic that transcended the bounds of race, color, or creed. His decision to move to Boston University hinged on the fact that as his students moved on from the University, what he taught would be spread to the far reaches of the world. Dean George and Thurman soon found their two realms overlapping, as they both shared, according to Sue Bailey Thurman, a "special interest in working with students as individuals, planning programs and activities emanating from their several departments." Often Sargent students enlivened the services at Marsh Chapel with interpretive ritual dances of "Deep River," "Go Down Moses," and other worshipful music. Thurman reciprocated by frequently appearing at Sargent Camp. Sue Bailey Thurman recalls that exciting time, and remembers that such activities "brought their respective departments together in a centric search for wholeness and for common ground."

As the 1950s came to a close, Dean George was settling into a steady course at Sargent College. His direction, however, was shifted at the close of the summer, when he was asked by President Case to also serve as acting dean of the School of Fine and Applied Arts. What he initially thought would be only a short stint turned into a two-year position. At the end of a successful period of leadership at SFAA, Dean George turned down the opportunity to serve permanently as dean there to return to Sargent full-time.

The 1960s, though increasingly turbulent on campus, brought his vision for the college to fulfillment. By the time Dean George reached the mandatory retirement age of sixty-five, in 1972, the college had evolved from being primarily a physical education school for women to a coeducational center of learning for the allied health professions, encompassing physical and occupational therapy and related areas at the undergraduate and graduate levels. Among other contributions, Dean George played a central part in the Massachusetts State Association for

*Viewing the sesquicentennial
parade of the Battle of Lexington: (lower right) George
with his grandfather, George
Makechnie; (above) his grandmother, Sarah Makechnie; (to
her left) his mother, Mabel
Makechnie. 1925.*

Health, Physical Education, and Recreation, his leadership including two terms as president. He also chaired several committees for the American Association for Health, Physical Education, and Recreation, and was a founding member of the American Society of Allied Health Professions. Over the years he was honored for his work by the American College of Sports Medicine; the Massachusetts State Association for Health, Physical Education, and Recreation; the American Physical Therapy Association; and many other such organizations.

Upon retiring, Dean George and Anne travelled to Europe to visit old friends and colleagues, most of whom he knew from earlier visits to England (to deliver addresses at Oxford for the British Association for Organizers and Lecturers in Physical Education, 1953 and 1963), Paris, and Copenhagen (for a physical therapy program he organized in 1963). After their return to the states, Dean George intentionally stayed away from the University to give his successor, Dean Bernard Kutner, space to establish his reign. Kutner, in turn, interpreted the distance as disapproval. Learning that, Dean George went in one day to meet with him and walked out with an assignment. With the centennial celebration of the founding of the Sargent School and the fiftieth anniversary of the gift from Ledyard Sargent to the University just around the bend, who better to chronicle the history of Sargent College than one who had been there?

Dean George's historical work, *Optimal Health: The Quest,* was published in 1979. In recognition of the book and of his fifty years of service to Boston University, he was awarded the degree Doctor of Humane Letters, *honoris causa,* at a University convocation. In his remarks, President Silber saluted Dean George by saying,

> Sargent College of Allied Health Professions will be forever linked in our minds with you, George Makechnie, for you are a founder and a leader in that profession: it was your forethought and your courageous conviction that the part does not function except in its proper relation to the whole which resulted in the successful integration of Sargent College and Boston University. Thus you went beyond *corpore sano* to the *mens sana* that is the essence of the University.

The early 1980s were marked by bereavement. In the fall of 1980, Anne died. The spring of 1981 brought another blow: his soulmate, Howard

Thurman, passed away. Concerned friends and family worried that Dean George would not be able to handle these tremendous losses. Yet the lesson his mother had taught him so many years ago — to find strength in adversity — stood him in good stead. In 1982, during a trip to San Francisco, Dean George accompanied a young friend to a Sunday-morning mass. As his vision shifted from the ornate marble fixtures at the base of the altar to the simple image of Jesus, arms outstretched, at the front of the chapel, he became inspired, his new mission clear. He had been pondering the best way to preserve the ideas of Howard Thurman. The way, then, was to spread the universal message of this man — the love ethic, which breaks through barriers of divisiveness.

Just as Thurman had decided two decades earlier that the best way to disseminate his thought was to serve in a university community, Dean George decided that Boston University must be a dynamic part of the Thurman legacy. He soon established the Howard Thurman Fellowship, which commemorated him at services twice a year, at the times of his birth (November) and death (April). In 1984, Sue Bailey Thurman gave the Howard Thurman Archive to Boston University. Soon after, in 1986, the Howard Thurman Center was established in an effort to involve students in his legacy even more. The center houses audio and video tapes of Thurman and serves as homebase for outreach programs to area prisons and pre-release centers. Since its inception, Dean George has served as director. Sue Bailey Thurman notes, "the spirit of Howard and George's collective efforts permeated the campus and beyond, leaving the encircling air of community which remains today as a part of the exciting life and work of the Howard Thurman Center." As an extension of his work at the center and at the request of Sue Bailey Thurman, Dean George wrote the book *Howard Thurman: His Enduring Dream,* published in 1988.

Today Dean George is still a presence on campus. He helps orient students in the fall and greets reunioning alumni in the spring. His office door is always open, as it was when he was dean. His work with the Thurman Center is ongoing, and his writing career is flourishing.

In telling the story of George Makechnie, it is impossible to separate Boston University from his life. His mark on the University is apparent: the atrium and the Instructional Resource Center in the Sargent

College building are named for him. The Thurman Center thrives as a part of the Office of the Dean of Students. He is often quoted in University publications that require a historical perspective. He is officially honored with the title "Dean Emeritus" and affectionately by successive generations of students as "Dean George." Over the years he has personally helped those struggling financially and has offered caring, solid counsel. He has indelibly impressed thousands of students, whose wedding albums and graduation pictures are illuminated with his smile. He is, as his long-time assistant Barbara McMahon once stated, "a true BU man."

Seventy years ago, George Kinsley Makechnie chose a path of learning and service at Boston University. His memoirs are testimony to his life choices, which are interwoven in the fabric of the history of Boston University. Thirty-five years ago, Dean George expressed the joy of his choices in a poem he entitled "Not the Least of These Memories."

> *Lay up for yourselves — Treasures*
> *How precious the possession*
> *of the moments of our days!*
> *The privilege of decisions — choosing*
> *that with which our moments will be filled —*
> *What a singular grace from the God of Life.*
>
> *Lay up for yourselves — Treasures*
> *Treasures of memory*
> *Treasures of act*
> *Treasures of vision*
> *Treasures of fact.*
>
> *Not the transient*
> *Which crumble like clay*
> *In the day*
>
> *But enduring*
> *Fulfilling*
> *Guiding our way.*

70 *Stories*
about
Boston University

1 9 2 3 – 1 9 9 3

President Daniel L. Marsh.

*President Marsh holds an
architect's rendering of the
tower that he envisioned as the
centerpiece of the developing
campus.*

The Daniel L. Marsh Era

I.   Daniel L. Marsh Takes the Helm

II. A Physically Strong and Optimistic Captain

III. My Appointment as Assistant to Dean Arthur H. Wilde: A First Step to Becoming Dean of Sargent College

IV. Today's Site of Mugar Memorial Library Was a Cow Pasture

V.   Serving as Executive Secretary of the Harvard–Boston University Extension Program, or Acquiring Obesity in Classical Academic Style

VI. Optimism: Denouement; Depression: Comes on Stage

VII. Captain Marsh Hits a Reef

VIII. Vote Your Hopes Instead of Your Fears

IX. A Funny Thing Happened on the Way to the Forum — No, No, to Our Wedding: A Daniel L. Marsh "Shocker" or Two

X.   Dean Wilde's Sixteen-Year Tenure Concludes with His Retirement in 1934; Jesse B. Davis Becomes Dean; Enter, Nursing Education

XI. Life During Wartime
     A. Marsh Responds to the Demands of War
     B. A Family's Experience with the Nazi Terror Brings the Horror Closer to Home

C. The Civil Affairs Training School; Hitler's Predecessor, Heinrich Brüning, Chancellor of the German Reich 1930–1932, Joins Our Faculty

D. It Can't Happen Here — Or Can It?

XII. General of the Army Dwight David Eisenhower Pays Tribute to Daniel L. Marsh on the Occasion of the Twentieth Anniversary of His Presidency

XIII. With Lightning Speed, Marsh Names Me Dean of Sargent College

XIV. A Wife's Honest Reaction

XV. Under Threat of Buckshot, My Deanship Begins

XVI. Marsh Shows a Flair for Drama

XVII. Marsh, the Lonely but Determined Leader

XVIII. The Opening in 1948 of What Is Today the College of Communication, and a Havana Cigar

XIX. Hell Is Paved with Good Intentions: Founders' Day 1949

XX. Anna Hiss

XXI. *Oratio ad Collectam* Delivered Solo

XXII. Marsh and I Visit the Chapel During Its Construction

XXIII. Marsh "Dips into the Future": Post-War Planning

XXIV. Marsh Still in Command in the Year of His Retirement

The Daniel L. Marsh Era

I. Daniel L. Marsh Takes the Helm

IT WAS A MILD WINTER'S DAY in late January 1926. Having responded to the command "at ease," the Reserve Officers Training Corps unit was standing beside the Boston Arena on St. Botoloph Street prior to entering the Boston University gymnasium section of that building to attend an assembly. I, a freshman with the lowly rank of private, was in that unit. On the sidewalk was a man of impressive bearing, observing us. Nudging a fellow private, I whispered, "That man over there looks very much like the picture of the new president of the University I saw in the Sunday paper. I'll bet it is he." It was. Daniel Marsh was about to give his first address to a Boston University audience: the ROTC. He would assume the presidency of Boston University in February.

That Marsh's first audience was the ROTC is interesting, if not a bit ironic. In the wake of World War I, opinion on campus was sharply divided about the propriety of ROTC as a University offering. At one extreme there were those who believed that it should be a requirement for all male students; at the other extreme were those who held that it had no place in the curriculum. Everett W. Lord, dean of the College of Business Administration, was firmly in the former group. Supported by most of his faculty, he insisted that all male students take ROTC for two years and that those desiring to become officers continue for two more years. Early in his administration, Marsh, reflecting his personal conviction, ruled that ROTC be an elective and not a required experience for any student. Dean Lord did not readily acquiesce to the new policy. Instead, he made the alternatives to ROTC so tough that few students chose to take them. The ranks of ROTC continued to be full. The ROTC issue continued to rankle, even more vehemently, during the terms of Marsh's successors.

Immediately following the assembly, I went to my class in public speaking, which was taught by English Professor William Hoffman of the College of Business Administration. He used the hour to analyze Marsh's address, which he found to be an exemplary model both in substance and in style of delivery. While specific details of that address have long since departed from memory, the positive impact of my first impression of Daniel Marsh translated itself into respectful admiration, which abides to this day.

What a capricious flight of fancy would have been required on that January day in 1926 for me, a freshman-private in ROTC, to imagine that twenty-five years later Daniel Marsh, approaching retirement, would invite me and a fellow dean to engage in a radio program with him to reminisce on his long tenure as president of Boston University (see p. 43).

The ceremonial inauguration of President Marsh took place at Boston's Symphony Hall on May 15, 1926. In his address on that occasion, Marsh likened the University to a ship, with the president as its captain, the charter as its sailing orders, and its port of destination "unselfish service for the sake of others." Expanding on the imagery of the University as a ship, he promised:

> *unselfish service to the city, the state, the nation, and the world;*
> *service to young men and young women,*
> *and to older ones as well;*
> *service to individuals, and to groups, and to society;*
> *service, unselfish service, for the sake of others —*
> *and at that port, we will aim continuously to deliver our cargo.*

In that address he also admonished against what he deemed to be a rising tide of materialism. He warned of dangers "lurking upon the rocks and reefs, and dangerous shoals of materialism." He expressed his fear of their effects on students, in particular. He lamented, "We are in peril of judging a student wholly on his ability to accumulate credits . . . and forgetting that a student's character, purpose, and spirit are of more worth than his credits, clothes, social position, and ancestry." Good sense and lofty purpose combined to be the theme of Marsh's inaugural message, which he expounded with a colorful imagery, a zeal, and a persuasiveness born of the ministerial background from whence he came.

II. A Physically Strong and Optimistic Captain

W HEN PRESIDENT MARSH assumed the formidable task of administering a disunified and geographically scattered University in 1926, he did so with characteristic optimism. His positive mood, although perpetually his personal hallmark, was at that time generally shared by his colleagues. The mood of the entire country was one of optimism. The year marked a high point in the post–World War I prosperity of the dizzy 1920s.

A disunified and geographically scattered institution was not the only problem that faced the new president. He was also haunted by a University debt of $425,000. Marsh used his "bully pulpit" to awaken the University, which had been called a "sleeping giant," to the crucial need to raise funds, if the schools and colleges were to be unified on the new campus.

The president was beginning to get some support when, alas, on October 29, 1929, the stock market crashed. That disaster dried up financial resources of potential donors. When the Great Depression of the 1930s followed in the wake of the stock market crash, Marsh experienced the loneliness of leadership: only he would have believed that funds could be raised and that new buildings would be erected on the new campus. "It will not happen in our lifetime" was the oft-repeated opinion in the faculty lounges and conference rooms. Neither trustees, administrators, nor faculty would share Marsh's unbelievable optimism that the deed could be done (see p. 43). Still Marsh, the optimistic captain of the ship, commanded himself and urged the rest of us to "sail on." By 1932, decreased enrollments and diminished returns from investments had drastically reduced the University's income, and Marsh responded by taking steps, some of which were painful to him.

Marsh brought to the demanding tasks of the University presidency extraordinary physical strength and stamina. On cold days when the snow was deep, he delighted in climbing to the top of Mt. Washington on snowshoes. In the privacy of his home, he would astound his friends by lifting a heavy chair and holding it at arm's length with one hand. Daily he walked to and fro between his home, the Castle on Bay State Road, and his office in Copley Square, until the move to the "New Campus." In inclement weather, he would recite to himself and any others who would listen the lines of the Hoosier poet James Whitcomb Riley:

> *It hain't no use to grumble and complain*
> *It's just as cheap and easy to rejoice.*
> *When God sorts out the weather*
> *And sends the rain*
> *W'y, rain's my choice.*

He boasted of his ability to cast off all cares at bedtime and fall immediately into a refreshing sleep. Nor would he worry about that about which he could do nothing. Often he would counsel us to follow his example. He would quote an old English proverb:

> *For every evil under the sun*
> *There's a remedy*
> *Or there's none.*
> *If there be one*
> *Try and find it*
> *If there be none — never mind it.*

During his long tenure, he often dealt with a disappointing experience by reminding himself that "if I cannot realize my ideal, I'll strive to idealize my real."

Thus the man of strength, stamina, emotional equanimity, and driving purpose tackled the basic problem of unifying a widely scattered

University — geographically scattered over the city of Boston from Beacon Hill to the South End, with its center at Copley Square and with its schools and colleges duplicating one another's offerings and, in some instances, competing with one another for students. The unification of the University was an ideal he determined to make real. The realization of that ideal, particularly in bricks and mortar, would become the signature of the Marsh administration. As the University charter provided Marsh's "sailing orders," so the by-laws defined his duties. Many described his administrative style as authoritarian, usually softening the phrase by adding "benevolently so." Such a style fit well with his temperament and with the prevailing by-laws.

III. My Appointment as Assistant to Dean Arthur H. Wilde: A First Step to Becoming Dean of Sargent College

In the academic year 1925–1926, I was a freshman in what was then called the "College of Business Administration." I acquired some skills there that would later serve me well as an administrator. Having a primary interest in teaching and being intrigued by the program Arthur H. Wilde, founding dean of the School of Education, had developed, I transferred to that school at the beginning of my sophomore year.

Wilde was a man of warmth and integrity. Unlike some other deans in schools of education, he was an academic scholar. As founding dean of the school, his intent was to provide liberal education to graduates of the two- and three-year normal school curricula, which were technical in nature. Often I would hear him counseling students to take courses in philosophy with Edgar Brightman; history with Warren Ault, Frank Novak, and Robert Moody; mathematics with Robert Bruce; and English with Everett Getchell. Although it was not a degree requirement, he urged students to include a foreign language among their courses. Before the establishment of the School of Education in 1918, Wilde had been professor of education in the College of Liberal

Arts, teaching courses in the history of education and educational psychology. Daniel L. Marsh had been Wilde's student in history when Wilde was a professor of history at Northwestern University.

A few weeks prior to my graduation, in June 1929, the dean proposed that in September I enroll for half-time graduate study and work for him the other half. Knowing that I had been offered a teaching position in an excellent private institution, he pointed out that a graduate degree was becoming increasingly a requirement for advancement in the profession. The master's degree could be earned in two years on a half-time schedule. He asked that I consider his proposal, and if I accepted it, let him know how much money I would need to meet basic expenses. I returned the next day to accept the offer. I informed him that I would need $700 each of the two years to cover essential needs. When the first check came, I was pleasantly surprised to find that it was based on the amount of $900 — not bad remuneration at that time.

In 1931, Wilde gave me the title "assistant to the dean," with the academic rank of instructor. The salary was fabulous: $1,800! Arthur Wilde was a mentor who by precept and example taught me much about the art of teaching and even more about the principles and techniques of administration: how to experience its fulfilling joys and how to cope with its irksome woes. Well do I remember his sharing with me his techniques and his values. Early on he told me: "Except in matters that must be kept confidential, such as a professor's salary, I try to operate in a manner that the world might know of my actions." His business acumen won the admiration of the University's treasurer, E. Ray Speare, who once told me, "It's astounding: Wilde was trained in history, theology, and music, but he is the sharpest business manager of any dean on the campus."

The saga leading to my becoming dean of Sargent College began when I became assistant to Dean Wilde, and he named me liaison with Sargent College and Sargent Camp. While still a student, in 1928–1929, I had performed tasks for the dean. During semester breaks, sometimes with him and more often alone, I talked in assemblies at Massachusetts "normal schools," which were then two- or three-year teacher training institutions. My topic related to the rewards of higher education for personal growth as well as financial remuneration. Of course, the intent of these visits was to recruit students for degree study in education.

One day during the first week in April 1929, Wilde asked me to substitute for him in an assembly at the Sargent School, which at that time was a proprietary school with a three-year curriculum to train women students in physical education. The dean showed me a letter from Ledyard Sargent, who had succeeded his late father, Dudley Allen Sargent, founder of the school. The letter was an urgent request that Dean Wilde address an assembly of the school about higher education generally and specifically about the increasing demand that applicants for teaching positions have baccalaureate degrees. For Sargent School graduates who would continue their studies in the School of Education, the dean had worked out a formula containing a variant relating to their academic position in their class. Wilde said to me, "You know that I dislike speaking in public, much more so to 350 girls; will you do it for me?" When, dear reader, you subtract from my age today, eighty-six, those sixty-four intervening years back to 1929, will you find it astonishing that a less-than-bashful youth of twenty-two would respond, "Yes, Dean Wilde, I'll do it for you"?

One week after the assembly, Ledyard Sargent and his wife, Etta, came to the School of Education to confer with the dean. Before entering his office, they chatted with me and thanked me for giving the address. Soon after the conference began, the dean invited me to join them. In a gruff and uncharacteristic voice, Wilde asked me, "Whatever did you say at the Sargent School last week?" Fearing that I had let go with an unacceptable Scottish profanity, I gazed at the floor. What a relief it was to be quickly shown a letter (which to this day I remember was on light blue stationery) that proposed the tender of Sargent School, its buildings, its curriculum program, and its goodwill, to Boston University. At the meeting of the trustees' executive committee the next month, the University accepted the gift. Thus, since May 1929, what is today called the Sargent College of Allied Health Professions has been a college at Boston University.

So also on that date began my sixty-plus-year relationship to Sargent College: a saga charged with human drama — the trials and tribulations of administration as well as the gratifying pleasantries of accomplishment, and, oh yes, that special elation that courtship and marriage alone can give.

On his acquiring administrative responsibility for Sargent College, Wilde named me liaison between the school, Sargent Camp, and the University. As liaison, I naturally had conferences with the president of the Student Council, Anne Schonland, who was also a student in my classes. She became my wife on her graduation day, June 12, 1993 (see p. 16).

There were other experiences — first as an administrative assistant and later as a director of the undergraduate program while teaching, the latter moving through the traditional stages from instructor to professor, that led to the deanship — some of which are revealed in the vignettes that follow.

IV. Today's Site of Mugar Memorial Library Was a Cow Pasture

IN 1929 AND THE EARLY 1930s, one of my assignments was to go once each week to what we called "New Campus" to ascertain the needs of the three faculty members and twenty-six students in the Art Department of the School of Education. Their needs were for pencils and paper, not for word processors and computers. They were housed in an old building near the Charles River, a tidal stream at that time. Before going to them, I would pause to pat three cows tethered to poles where Mugar Library stands today. The area was called "Cottage Farm," and today's "Boston University Bridge" was "Cottage Farm Bridge."

President Murlin, predecessor of Marsh and under whose administration the land was purchased, described that land that is today the Charles River Campus as being sufficiently close to the city, but "possessing some rural charm." When later the College of Business Administration would be evicted from its quarters near Copley Square and President Marsh would insist that it be moved to the "New Campus," its dean, Everett W. Lord, protested, saying: "It's ridiculous to take a school of business out into the country." But Marsh prevailed (see p. 44).

V. Serving as Executive Secretary of the
Harvard–Boston University Extension Program
or
Acquiring Obesity in Classical Academic Style

ANOTHER OF MY EARLY assignments was to serve as executive secretary for the University's Connecticut Valley Division, which was a branch of the School of Education located in Springfield. When the division was merged with the Harvard–Boston University Extension Course program, I became both a faculty member and an administrative assistant in the extension program. John J. Mahoney was its director. He was a Harvard graduate and the first person whom Dean Wilde appointed to the faculty of the School of Education when it was established in 1918.

In the way that disparate elements may combine to produce curious results, so the Harvard–Boston University Extension Course program contributed to an interval during which my bathroom scales warned: uh oh! To make the scenario almost implausible, Abbott Lawrence Lowell, then president of Harvard University, played a key role in the drama. On one of his visits to President Lowell to discuss the extension program, Mahoney took me to Harvard with him. Entering the president's office, we found him in a mood of savory contentment. He told us that he had just returned from one of the dormitory kitchens, where he had sampled delicious muffins fresh from the oven. He explained: "Each morning I make it a point to visit one or another dormitory. Tasting the fresh food, I enthusiastically compliment the cook." He went on to say that he had learned that his visits to the kitchens and his expressions of approval of the cooks' culinary expertise assured fine food for the students. When I became dean of Sargent College and administrator ("housefather") of the dorms, I followed Lowell's example. (*Transformations: A History of Boston University,* p. 200, provides in pictorial form twenty extra pounds of corpulent evidence of my own "transformation.")

VI. Optimism: Denouement
Depression: Comes on Stage

THE 1920s ENDED WITH a spirit of optimism running high. French doctor Coué cheered our spirits, proclaiming that "every day in every way, we're getting better and better." Of course we thought so and responded: "Is not the 1929 Buick better than the 1928 model? Then so will the 1930 one be better still." Fatalistic and spontaneous progress was the prevailing mood of the decade. But the 1930s came and with them, a worldwide economic depression. The U.S. president, Herbert Hoover, tried hard to persuade himself and the rest of us that "prosperity was just around the corner" and that there would soon be "a two-car garage in every yard and a chicken in every pot." But no, instead "hard times came a knockin' at the door." Very hard times. By 1932, the Depression had made deep inroads on the higher education system, including Boston University. Marsh, while keeping his undying sense of optimism, dealt with the new problem with characteristic forthrightness and Wilde, with seasoned "business acumen."

During the depression years the president called for cuts in the operational budgets of the schools and colleges. Responding to one such order, Dean Wilde shared with me how he handled "cuts" for the School of Education. He was well aware that, even during the depression years, the school's income was well in excess of its expenses. He showed me a copy of the proposal he had submitted to the president, which met the demand for a cut of 15 percent. I was astounded by it. He had eliminated part-time course offerings, which were taught evenings and Saturday mornings by outstanding authorities in their respective fields. Drs. Healy and Bronner headed the Judge Baker Foundation, which dealt with problems of children. They taught a course called "Child Growth and Development," which had enrolled over one hundred students each year. Compensation to the instructors was $300. At a tuition rate of $20 per semester hour, the course produced an income in excess of $2,000. A course taught by Cheney Jones, director of the New England Home for Little Wanderers, fell into the same category, and there were others.

The president accepted the dean's proposal. Whereupon the dean submitted another. He now proposed that those courses that he had eliminated in the first instance be reinstated with the proviso that they return an income in excess of expense or be cancelled. He calculated that an enrollment of twenty students would do that with a comfortable margin of gain. Again the president approved and the fall term opened with a full complement of courses being offered and the entire full- and part-time faculties intact. In fact, none of the classes enrolled fewer than eighty students. In later years, when I was a dean or acting dean, and even today as dean emeritus, Wilde's counsel, his example, and his administrative skills continue to tutor me.

Did Dean Wilde's ghost hover over budget maneuvers when later "deaning" fell to my lot? Perhaps that ghost even today is the wisp that fleets about in time of need. I think so.

In the way that life's experiences, whether painful or pleasant, contain those humorous touches that lift our spirits and help us bear even grim ordeals, so a touch of levity lightened our receiving Marsh's announcement about salary cuts. One day Marsh called a meeting of the faculty and staff. I was standing near Arthur Metcalf and an older faculty member. The president opened the meeting by telling us how much he loved us — a teardrop rolled down his cheek. Metcalf and I were moved by the president's expression of concern for us. The more seasoned older professor warned us, saying: "Where there is so much love, someone is about to be screwed!" We were about to be informed of a cut in salary. It would be followed by other cuts, and before the Depression was over, the total reduction became 19 percent.

A decision that Marsh courageously made related to the older faculty, many of whom were his close friends. Convinced that the University's future was dependent upon the retention of its younger faculty members, Marsh ordered the retirement of older members with a pension of $700 annually. This move was painfully distasteful to Marsh, but he made it to assure the University's well-being into the years beyond his presidency.

VII. Captain Marsh Hits a Reef

IN THE ACADEMIC YEAR 1931–1932, I was president of the local chapter of Phi Delta Kappa, an honor society in the field of education. In that capacity I presided at a dinner meeting to which guests were invited, including members of the trustees' standing committee for the School of Education. Among the trustees who accepted the invitation was Mrs. James Storrow. She would later provide funds in memory of her husband to create a basin in the Charles River and to build a highway — Storrow Drive — along the river's bank. Mrs. Storrow had informed me that she would be a little late but to be sure not to delay serving the dinner on her account.

President Marsh, a member of the society, requested that I not call on him to speak before Mrs. Storrow arrived. Believing that he wished to extend a cordial greeting to her as a trustee, I, of course, agreed. Soon after he began to speak, I wanted to crawl under the table. He spoke about the University's dire need for money and, aiming his remarks directly at Mrs. Storrow, he said (and these are almost his exact words): "Only when good friends with the resources, good friends like Mrs. Storrow, come to our aid will we have smooth sailing." The good ship "Boston University" hit a reef. Mrs. Storrow's flushed face portrayed her resentment.

The next morning, Mrs. Storrow visited Dean Wilde. She spoke a pleasant word to me before going into his office. She told the dean of her embarrassed distress and that she had just submitted her resignation as a trustee. However, she said she would continue to support the dean, which she did. Reflecting her deep interest in the Boy and Girl Scout movements, she paid all the expenses to send Dean Wilde and his wife to England, where she had arranged for a lengthy conference for the dean with Lord Baden-Powell, founder of the scouting movement. Mrs. Storrow expressed her belief that the School of Education could and should play a significant role in the movement in the United States.

Lord Baden-Powell recommended that Major Maur, a highly skilled scouting leader in England, be given a twelve-month contract to teach and demonstrate at the School of Education and at Sargent Camp.

This was done. Mrs. Storrow gave the money for his salary and related expenses. His work was well received.

Even today, at reunions, alumni proudly demonstrate their knotting ability and tell me that they learned the skills in Major Maur's classes so long ago.

Perhaps it was inevitable that Marsh's super-enthusiasm for building the University would run afoul of an occasional riptide or current. Such incidents detracted for a moment from his demonstrated navigational skill.

VIII. Vote Your Hopes Instead of Your Fears

VOTE YOUR HOPES instead of your fears" was the campaign slogan of Norman Thomas, Socialist candidate for president of the United States in the depression year 1932. He accepted an invitation to speak in Jacob Sleeper Hall at Boston University. Edgar Brightman was among those who arranged the meeting. I volunteered to drive Thomas from the Hotel Bellevue, on Beacon Hill, to the University, near Copley Square.

My car was a Nash with bucket front seats. Anne, then my fiancée, accompanied me. When Thomas joined me in the hotel lobby, two men jumped up and followed us. They were forbidding looking, badly dressed and of grim countenance. Getting into the bucket seat with Anne, Thomas, a tall and robust man, addressed the two men: "You guys get in the back seat; I'm sitting in front with my friends." I wondered: If the likes of these men are Socialists, are Anne and I making a bad mistake in supporting Thomas?!

At the intersection of Boylston and Exeter Streets, the men ordered me to park directly in front of Jacob Sleeper Hall. But the traffic cop screamed, "Move that car! You know you can't park there." Much as I feared the good officer of the law, I feared the two "thugs" more. The car stayed parked.

Soon we learned that the men were neither thugs nor Socialists. They were Boston's finest plainclothesmen. The police had learned that a plot to assassinate Norman Thomas was timed to take place while he was riding with us!

Woodrow Wilson's daughter, Jessie Sayre, invited Anne and me, along with others who were planning to vote for Thomas, to a semi-secret meeting at the Hotel Lenox. There, Felix Frankfurter, a Harvard Law School professor and later a Supreme Court justice, told us that Franklin Roosevelt, if elected, would recognize the Soviet Union diplomatically and take the country off the "sacred" gold standard. If Roosevelt announced these intentions in "sound bites" or the equivalent thereof at that time, it would turn off thousands of voters who feared the Soviet Union and revered the gold standard.

Perhaps Thomas's candidacy softened the blow. Roosevelt did recognize the Soviet Union, and he did take the country off the gold standard. And perhaps Thomas won: the New Deal resembled his program in many ways, but he didn't have to carry the awesome burden of the presidency.

IX. A Funny Thing Happened on the Way to the Forum —
No, No, to Our Wedding:
A Daniel L. Marsh "Shocker" or Two

ON FEBRUARY 22, 1933, Anne's stepmother announced our engagement at a meeting of Honor Auxiliary, a Sargent College society of which Anne was president. In accordance with the social custom of that time, a notice of the engagement was sent to relatives and friends. President and Mrs. Marsh received the notice, whereupon he invited me to visit with him.

No, he didn't say what today would be said: "George, you are fired for dating one of your students." On the contrary, he congratulated me on my good fortune. How strange we mortals are. That which was blessed in the more prudish 1930s is condemned in the more permissive 1990s. Shakespeare had the insight: "There is nothing either good or bad, but thinking makes it so."

Marsh proceeded to tell me that he had come to know Anne as a student leader and that he was very fond of her. Then, bringing into play his sense of the significance of symbols, he said: "Just think of how meaningful it would be to have the wedding on Anne's graduation day, June 12th." We had, however, chosen June 17, Bunker Hill Day. At that time, June 17 was a holiday in Massachusetts celebrated with the completeness of that of the 4th of July. In 1933, the state and the nation were in the grips of the Depression. Employers were using every excuse possible to reduce personnel. The holiday would enable people, particularly men, to attend the wedding without fear that absenteeism would jeopardize their jobs.

Depression-induced financial straits were being experienced by countless families, including Anne's. Thus, she sent only handwritten wedding invitations to friends. The letter to the Marshes and others stated that the service would take place on June 17, 1933, at the Universalist Church in Lawrence, Massachusetts—the church of Anne's childhood.

Suddenly our plans changed. A demand arose for a course that I taught to be offered in June. Grateful for the extra compensation, which would enable Anne and me to buy a refrigerator, I agreed to teach the class. The new teaching assignment made Monday, June 12, the more appropriate date for our wedding. Having the wedding on June 12 gave me the added privilege of handing Anne her diploma in the morning Commencement. Commencement Day would also be a University holiday, with classes cancelled. We could have a brief honeymoon on a two-day round trip on the boat to Bangor, Maine. Why not a quiz for the class on Tuesday? I would be back in class on Wednesday, June 14. That is precisely what happened. Our wedding was to take place in the University's Robinson Chapel, in the School of Theology building on Mount Vernon Street, on Beacon Hill. Dr. Guy Robbins, Anne's childhood minister, would officiate. But a funny thing happened, not on "the way to the forum" but to Beacon Hill. In her letter notifying the Marshes of the change of date, Anne expressed the hope that the new time would be convenient for them to attend the service as guests.

On Friday evening, June 9, the Sargent College senior class had a graduation dance at the Woodland Golf Club in Newton. Anne and I attended. So also did Dr. and Mrs. Marsh. It was their much-appreciated custom to spend a few minutes at such events conducted by students of the different schools and colleges.

When they arrived, they hastened to find Anne and me. As the intensity of an experience will be etched indelibly in memory, so I remember today with amusement what transpired to our consternation that evening so long ago. Marsh asked if we would be willing to begin the wedding ceremony a half hour later than the three o'clock time that had been scheduled. He reminded us that he and Mrs. Marsh would be host and hostess at the Commencement luncheon at the Algonquin Club, and that they would be just breaking up at 3:00 p.m. I pointed out that, as it was, we would have barely enough time to get to the boat, which would sail from the Port of Boston at 5:00. Then came a Marsh shocker: "How disappointed will you both be, if I cannot do it?" At once I realized that he meant "perform the ceremony." He had interpreted the change of locale from the Universalist Church in Lawrence to the University's chapel as an indication that he would preside at the wedding.

The wheels of my brain, which often move slowly on their axes, were spurred into whirlwind speed. I replied: "Let's leave it this way; we'll have Dr. Guy Robbins, Anne's minister, take charge [of course, we had made the arrangement with Robbins weeks before] and if you can make it, we will ask him to give you a significant part in the service." Marsh said, "That's an excellent solution; we shall try to be with you."

After a brief visit with the president of the class, who brought the gathering to quiet attention, Marsh greeted the guests with his customary salutation: "Good friends, all." He went on to wish them well at graduation and in the "unknown years ahead." Anne and I went out on the cool, green grass and collapsed in relief — agitated relief — grateful that an otherwise extremely embarrassing situation had been resolved satisfactorily.

If the "shocker" at the Golf Club were not enough, another was to follow as Anne and her family were literally on their way to the wedding. Anne was driven to Beacon Hill by her brother-in-law, Blair Thompson. Also in the car were her father, sister, and stepmother, whom we called "Aunt Mattie" because she was a relative of Anne's late mother. Aunt Mattie was a very high-strung person. She had fretted about the Marsh incident since hearing about it two days before. "What will Dr. Robbins do if Dr. Marsh appears?" and she conjured up every other worry imaginable. Just as Anne and family arrived at the chapel, the Marshes also drove up. Aunt Mattie was beside herself in panic. Anne later told me that she said, "Blair, go in quickly and tell George." Blair went. But Marsh, knowing a short cut, arrived at the minister's study first. I was introducing Marsh and Robbins when the door was flung open and my soon-to-be brother-in-law shouted, "Hey, George, Marsh is here." As the three of us laughed, I said, "Yes, Blair, let me introduce you to him."

The ceremony proceeded with quiet dignity, tempered by the simplicity appropriate in those prevailing hard times. John Patton Marshall, dean of the College of Music and one of the closest friends among my colleagues, was at the organ. During the ceremony itself, mutedly he played Mendelssohn's "Spring Song," a favorite of Anne's. Forty-seven years later, University organist Max Miller would play the same piece mutedly during the reading of the Twenty-Third Psalm at Anne's memorial service.

At our wedding, Marsh read the story of Ruth: "Thy people shall be my people and thy God, my God." And he gave the closing prayer. Always in command, following his "Amen," Marsh turned to me and, in a stage whisper heard by all present, said, "Kiss her, George." I did. Was it out of obedience to Marsh or because of natural instinct that I kissed Anne at that momentous instant?

You decide, dear reader.

Anne and I were profoundly grateful that Daniel Marsh would shorten the Commencement luncheon in 1933 to participate in our wedding ceremony. We were pleased that, although not a participant, Dean Wilde attended. So am I equally grateful that John Silber would rearrange important appointments in Washington, D.C., to be a participant in Anne's memorial service at Marsh Chapel in 1980.

X. Dean Wilde's Sixteen-Year Tenure Concludes
with His Retirement in 1934
Jesse B. Davis Becomes Dean
Enter, Nursing Education

ALTHOUGH IN THE EARLY 1930s there was no age requirement for retirement, when Dean Wilde reached the age of seventy, in 1934, he resigned, saying that he felt that the direction of the school should be in younger hands. Marsh named Jesse B. Davis, a member of the faculty since the school's founding in 1918, as dean. Ironically, he was only five years younger than Wilde. Davis would serve until 1941, when Donald D. Durrell became his successor.

Davis asked me to continue my teaching and become what he phrased a "teaching registrar." In that latter capacity, I had a role in a major development: the introduction of nursing education.

As registrar, I was surprised to discover that seventeen nurses had enrolled in the fall semester of 1937 in courses designed for teachers. Davis reported my finding to Marsh, who immediately commissioned me to explore the matter further. Margaret Dieter, superintendent of nurses at Massachusetts Memorial Hospitals (today, University Hospital), was the president of the Massachusetts chapter of the League of Nursing Education. In November 1937, I had a conference with her at the hospital.

At the end of an hour's discussion, Dieter asked that I submit to her in writing my question: "What, if anything, should Boston University do about nursing education?" She said that she would submit my question to the board of the league. Handing me a book entitled *Curriculum Guide for Schools of Nursing,* which had just been published by the National League of Nursing Education, she said: "I feel that a landmark in nursing education may have been reached this morning." She went on to point out that, with the exception of the Yale graduate school of nursing, nowhere else in New England could the league's guidelines be implemented, and since the Yale program was a graduate offering only and the majority of nurses were without baccalaureate degrees, they were not eligible for admission. She concluded by saying that she was reasonably sure that her board would respond favorably and that she

Cottage Farm Bridge (today, Boston University Bridge) and a section of today's Charles River Campus where, in the 1920s, cows grazed. 1950.

Above. "Who says that our dean he ain't got no style?" Michael Lannom, riflery instructor, waits for his turn in an English lawn ball match at Sargent Camp. 1947.

Daniel Marsh lays the cornerstone for the College of Business Administration building, the first construction on the Charles River Campus; (left to right) William Chenery, M.D., trustee; Everett Lord, dean of the College of Business Administration; Willard Hayden, director of the Charles Hayden Foundation; Frank Allen, chairman of the Boston University Board of Trustees; Bishop Lewis Hartman, trustee. 1938.

Above. Harvard University President James Conant, General of the Army Dwight Eisenhower, and President Daniel Marsh (left to right) celebrating the twentieth anniversary of Marsh's presidency of Boston University. 1946.

Arthur H. Wilde, dean of the School of Education from its founding in 1918 to 1934.

Left. Anne and George leaving Boston University's Robinson Chapel. June 12, 1933.

Below. Dean George with members of the Sargent College Student Camp Council discussing a plan for camping around the calendar. 1947.

Below. Anne and George at Nickerson Field in Weston one month before their wedding. 1933.

would appoint a committee to engage with me in a feasibility study. The members of the committee were among the top leaders, nationally as well as locally, in the field of nursing.

The committee met with me regularly for one year. Sometimes the sessions were held in the evening at our home. It was decided that a "trial balloon" course called "Current Trends in American Nursing," with nurse leaders of national reputation as lecturers, should be offered in the 1938 fall semester. If at least 35 students registered, it would be considered a positive indication that we should move ahead to develop a comprehensive program. Most members of the committee predicted an enrollment of 50. I assigned a room seating 125 persons for the first session.

The course was to begin on September 22. With no warning, and therefore no preparation, the 1938 New England hurricane wrought its massive destruction the day before the class was to start. "Gone with the Wind" was my troubled concern for the fate of our project. There were many personal injuries and nurses were in demand. To my utter amazement and that of the other committee members, ten minutes before the class was to begin I was forced to move the session to an auditorium: 196 nurses had registered!

The University responded quickly to the obvious demand for a program in nursing. On our recommendation, Marsh and the trustees authorized the establishment of a division of nursing education in the School of Education. I was commissioned to offer Martha Ruth Smith the position of administrative director and professor of nursing education. My conference with her was at the Massachusetts General Hospital, where she was happy as a tenured member of the staff. She did not want to leave her satisfying and secure position there. Tears flowed freely. But in due course she dried them and her words continue to this day to ring in my memory: "A nurse responds to the call of duty. I consider it my duty to accept the challenge implicit in your invitation. I am now fifty years old. I look forward to fifteen productive years at Boston University. You shall see no more tears."

Under her leadership, the program prospered. Quickly it achieved a national and international reputation for excellence. It laid the foundation for the establishment of the School of Nursing in 1946. The document recommending that the school be created was submitted by a committee of three appointed by Marsh. Martha Ruth Smith, Trustee Augustus P. Loring, Jr., and I were the members. The document was signed at Sargent Camp in June 1946. Continuing the reputation for excellence earned by the Division of Nursing Education, the school became recognized as the exemplary model for the nation. It held that reputation throughout the deanship of Smith's successor, Marie Farrell. Defining nursing as a profession in its own right, the school performed a lasting service by leading nursing away from its traditional, servile role into a more synergistic partnership with medicine. For that accomplishment alone, the Boston University School of Nursing earned an honored niche in the history of the profession.

Now a more-or-less humble confession: I moonlighted in the early 1940s. I taught courses outside Boston University for extra remuneration at Children's and Peter Bent Brigham hospitals, and gave commencement addresses *pro bono* at Beth Israel and other institutions. The "less" in my confession relates to a self-convincing justification: the promotion of the Boston University program, the exigencies of war, and, admittedly, help with mortgage payments for our home.

Nurses who served in the combat zones sometimes suffered lasting emotional scars inflicted by the frightening noises of battle. I taught a group of such "war-weary" nurses at the army hospital in Framingham. An officer warned me to be careful not to drop a book or do anything else to cause a sudden noise that might trigger the nurses' memory of gunfire in battle. In retrospect, teaching nurses during the World War II era ranks among the highly rewarding experiences of my long career.

XI. Life During Wartime

A. Marsh Responds to the Demands of War

THE JAPANESE AERIAL ATTACK at Pearl Harbor on December 7, 1941, shocked everybody to an acute awareness of the peril that faced the nation and, indeed, all the allies. France had fallen to the enemy. The Battle of Britain brought wrenching consequences. At that stage of the war, victory was more in the realm of hope than of certainty. On Monday, December 8, Marsh convened an assembly of the faculties and students to hear President Franklin Roosevelt's radio address to the nation. Following Roosevelt's stirring challenge, Marsh rose to the demands of inspiring leadership. He addressed us and declared: "Boston University as an institution and its component parts will do everything within its power to aid the United States government in bringing this war to a successful conclusion as quickly as possible, guaranteeing a durable peace built upon righteousness."

Soon he would demonstrate the gutsy character of his leadership. On a day when Marsh was out of town, the governor of the Commonwealth received an alert that German planes with a payload of bombs had been spotted heading for Boston. In the panic of the moment, the governor ordered the immediate evacuation of the city. A state of utter confusion ensued — vividly do I remember the experience. Warren Powell, the University's guidance counselor, and his wife, a member of the faculty, were passengers in my car. The traffic was so dense that we were stopped dead in our tracks on what is today called "Boston University Bridge." Stalled there for thirty minutes, we were sitting ducks for enemy bombs. We were terrified. After a few minutes, Warren broke the tension. He laughed, telling us that our situation was like one he had experienced in France some months before. We joined in the laughter when he said, "Look at me; I'm alive to tell the tale." Toward evening we learned that the scare had been a false alarm. The planes were not German but our own, carrying needed supplies to an inland city.

When Marsh returned the next day, our "captain" took command. Forcefully, he directed that Boston University would not again respond to such an ill-advised order, and he so informed the governor. He had "bomb shelters" designated in each building to which, in an orderly manner, we must go when an alert was sounded. Thereafter there were frequent air-raid drills. I was responsible for executing them in the Soden Building, which housed the School of Education, School of Music, and guidance offices.

As civilian-student enrollment declined, particularly because men were off to war, military-related enrollment increased. A variety of programs for the Army and Navy were instituted, including a specialized offering for Army Enlisted Reserves and the Navy V-1 program. Marsh named Professor Chester M. Alter of the Chemistry Department chairman of the Committee on War Relations.

B. A Family's Experience with the Nazi Terror Brings the Horror Closer to Home

A firsthand family experience with Hitler's inhumanity occurred in 1938. A German cousin of my wife, still living in Saxony, was married to a Jewish physician with many Aryan patients. But when Hitler became chancellor (he preferred the title "Der Führer"), anti-Semitism was rampant. Frightened, the doctor's Aryan patients ceased coming to his office. A final terrifying rumor that marriages between Aryans and Jews were to be dissolved brought Anne's cousin to Massachusetts to confer with the family about escaping to the United States. A requirement for the couple's immigration would be that they not become welfare-dependent here.

Happily, my work with the hospitals in Boston in the development of our nursing program gave me an in at Beth Israel Hospital. The physician was hired there as a laboratory assistant. While serving in that capacity, he prepared for and successfully passed examinations qualifying him to practice medicine in Massachusetts. Before World War II had ended, he had established a successful practice in Roxbury.

C. The Civil Affairs Training School Hitler's Predecessor, Heinrich Brüning, Chancellor of the German Reich 1930–1932, Joins Our Faculty

On October 4, 1943, I was called from teaching a class to report to the president's office. There I found Marsh; his assistant, John S. Perkins; Chester Alter; Elwood Hettrick, dean of the Law School; and a colonel of the United States Army who represented the provost marshall general. I was informed that the University had been granted one of ten contracts to conduct a Civil Affairs Training School to train senior officers of the United States Army for the allied military government operations in the European and Asiatic theaters of war. The other universities were the University of Chicago, Harvard University, University of Michigan, Northeastern University, University of Pittsburgh, Stanford University, Western Reserve University, University of Wisconsin, and Yale University. Of these, five, including Boston University, were assigned to the European theater and five, including Harvard University, to the Asiatic theater.

I was informed that I had been recruited to be chairman of Areas Studies and that Dr. Arthur Burkard, an authority on German art and architecture as well as a teacher of German language, would be chairman of Language Studies. They also informed me that upon completing the military aspects of their training at Fort Custer, the officers would arrive at Boston University on Monday, October 25, and that classes would begin on Wednesday, October 27. My task would be to complete the hiring of faculty and plan the curriculum following guidelines provided by the Office of the Provost Marshall General. All this in a period of three weeks — *mais, c'est la guerre!*

To be responsible for students who were senior officers in the Army would, indeed, be a novel experience for me, a faculty member and director of undergraduate studies in the School of Education. What would these men be like? Would they fit the stereotype: "This is the Army, Mr. Jones"? They soon dispelled my preconceived notions. They had been leaders in their respective fields in civilian life: one the attorney general of Oklahoma, another the lieutenant governor of Nebraska, others distinguished physicians, educators, journalists, business executives, bankers, and lawyers. They came equally from east and west of the Mississippi River and north and south of the Mason-Dixon line. None was younger than thirty or older than fifty. Two were lieutenant colonels, twenty-five were majors, thirty-seven were captains, and twenty-five were lieutenants.

The shortness of time notwithstanding, we were able to assemble a faculty of unusually appropriate qualifications. Among them were:

Heinrich Brüning, chancellor of the German Reich, 1930–1932; Robert Ulich, member of the Ministry of Education and supervisor of universities in Saxony, 1924–1933; Friederich von Koshembahr, educational officer in Saxony under Ulich, 1924–1933; Herbert Gezork, general secretary, Baptist Youth Movement in Germany, 1931–1934; Gerhard von Koshembahr, *Oberregierungsrat* (chief counsellor), Germany's Department of Railroads, 1914–1933; George Strassman, medical officer in the German Army, 1914–1918, *Professor extraordenarius,* legal and social medicine, Breslau University, and medical examiner in Breslau, 1928–1935; J. Anton DeHaas, professor in de Technich van den Handel, Handelschgeschule, Rotterdam, 1918–1921; Herbert C. Roth, First National Bank of Boston's representative in Europe, 1927–1941; Walter Kotschnig, director of the High Commission for Refugees from Germany, League of Nations, 1934–1936; Clair Turner, chairman, Department of Public Health, Massachusetts Institute of Technology; Karl Lowenstein, lecturer on constitutional and international law, University of Munich Law School, 1931–1933, and practicing attorney in the German courts; Henry Orne, practicing attorney in Vienna, 1921–1938; and Hans Apel, president of the largest German brewery, 1930–1933.

Others included: Ernest Pisko, editor-in-chief, *Wochenausgabe Neues Wiener Tageblatt,* Austria's leading democratic weekly, 1935–1938; Otto Zausmer, journalist in Vienna, 1928–1938; Albert Roy, publisher in Vienna, 1930–1936; Warren Ault, professor of history, Boston University, 1913–1957, professor emeritus, 1957–1989; Frank Novak, professor of history, Boston University, and United States delegate to the rededication of Poland, 1920; Norman Padelford, United States State Department representative and professor, Fletcher School, Tufts University; Kirtley Mather, professor, Department of Geology and Geography, Harvard University; Hans Kohn, professor of history, Smith College;

Colonel John Perkins, resident liaison officer between the University and the Provost Marshall General's Office.

While Austria, France, Belgium, and Holland were included in our assignment, we were instructed to concentrate upon Germany. Seven areas were to be covered in the curriculum: administration, jurisprudence, social structure (education, news media, and the mores generally), health, agriculture, transportation, and banking.

It is evident from the names on the faculty roll that the members were highly qualified as specialists in their respective areas. Through the good offices of Frederich von Koshembahr, I had been able to secure an appointment with Brüning, who at the outset of our visit informed me that he did not accept assignments that would give him politically related exposure. This was because of the hostage problem; his male secretary had been taken and assassinated, and his own sister was still in Germany. I described the nature of the Civil Affairs Training School and its mission, and assured him that all its personnel would be screened by the F.B.I. and would operate without publicity. After several moments of silent reflection, he said: "To have well-informed officers prepared to administer civil affairs in the occupied regions of Germany is so important to the future of my country that I will suspend my policy of nonparticipation and head your area of government studies."

Securing Heinrich Brüning to interpret the changing forms of government in Germany from the Treaty of Versailles to the rise of Nazism and the advent of Hitler was a coup of the first order. Brüning had been one of the architects of the Weimar Republic (1919–1933) and chancellor of the Reich during the period of Hitler's rise to power (1930–1932). Ousted from office by Germany's aging president, Paul von Hindenburg, who in his declining years was easily duped by Hitler, Brüning was first among those sought for execution in 1933, when Hitler became chancellor. Brüning fled Germany and in 1943 was at Harvard University in the Littauer Center, where I conferred with him.

Brüning and I had lunch together several times. He told me of his sessions with Adolph Hitler after the "beer-hall-putsch" in Munich. They would be alone together in the chancellor's large office on the Unter den Linden. Hitler would orate, waving his arms as he did when speaking to the throngs in Berlin and other cities. Brüning said: "I would let him rave on for a few minutes, then interrupt him with a simple question. Hitler would respond by deflating like a balloon pricked by a pin."

Brüning also told me of the perils he endured during his escape from the Nazis. He had been alerted to the existence of a list of one thousand people scheduled for assassination. His name was at the top. Out of loyalty — although cooperating with Hitler's regime as the path of least resistance — a few friends escorted him at night through woods and fields, over hills, and across valleys. After many nights, weary and bruised, they crossed the border into Holland. Between sheets for the first time in weeks, Brüning was awakened. His escort had discovered that the innkeeper was secretly a Nazi waiting for him. Brüning and his companions made a ladder from the sheets and other bedding and climbed down to begin the perilous march again. Suffering a heart condition, Brüning ultimately arrived in England, where he recuperated; later he came to the United States.

Well do I remember Brüning standing in my office doorway on the morning of November 6, 1943. He said: "Herr Professor Makechnie, I have just learned that last night your wife presented you with a beautiful daughter. Please give Mrs. Makechnie my greeting and kiss the baby for me." In an assembly the following week, the officers named Joan "Honorary Colonel" in their unit and presented me with a silver baby cup for her.

As Brüning brought firsthand experience at the highest level of government and gave a tone of reality to the school's offering, other faculty members made equally real and practical contributions in their respective spheres of expertise. Of special significance was the short-wave radio underground communication system developed by Otto Zausmer, which enabled him to pick up news reports, directives, and speeches being aired in Germany, even those given by Hitler himself. Thus our officers received the information and propaganda being broadcast in Germany.

Also of major significance was the contribution of Herbert Gezork, who in a scholarly and articulate manner interpreted the social customs of Germany. That the officers become aware of the difference in mores between the United States and Germany was highly important. A case in point: a young German member of the language faculty, who previously had been a student in my classes in the School of Education, once asked to talk to me "in confidence." He told me he was about to marry the daughter of an American industrialist. When I congratulated him on his good fortune, he responded sharply, saying: "No, I am marrying beneath my station; I am a teacher!" To find the most influential citizens of a town or city under allied occupation, our officers would need to single out the teacher or the preacher, not the captain of industry. Gezork made such facts abundantly clear.

The interpretation of German mores would be especially important for the general morale of the war-torn communities. Once the combat zone had been moved to a point beyond their border, citizens who had been exposed to the horrors of battle would need reassurance that their respected leaders were cooperating with the officers of occupation. All faculty members shared with the officers valuable information in the different areas of study, gained in firsthand experience.

From the first day of classes, each man was assigned to two teams: one of specialists and another of generalists. They were given problems that related to military government. Each officer would meet first with the team of his own specialty to study the problem from the perspective of that expertise. He would then join the other members of his generalist team, which would have the input from the other specialists to help solve the problem. Grades for promotion were in large degree based on performance in these problem-solving situations.

In the theaters of war, allied military government would be established in a territory after combat troops had advanced to a zone farther on. Fighting would have left destruction, disruption, and confusion within the communities in the zone just vacated by the troops. The task of the civil affairs officers would be to restore as much order and stability as possible, so that civilian life might go on.

While most of the problems assigned to the officers were based on imaginary situations in various areas of Germany, one was focused directly on Greater Boston. The local setting was chosen to give the officers firsthand experiences in "taking over" offices of government, education and the press, law, health, transportation, and banking. At the request of Colonel John Perkins, who was our liaison with the Office of the Provost Marshall General, I arranged to have officers of state government put "under arrest." Leverett Saltonstall was governor of the Commonwealth of Massachusetts. When I assured him that the whole exercise would be done without publicity, he was a good sport and readily agreed. His cooperation made it a cinch to get the consent of the secretaries for each of the areas in our program: administration, jurisprudence, transportation, agriculture, health, education, and social mores. The men were not aware that the governor and the secretaries were well informed about our plan. The problems that were to be solved by the men in their seven specialist and seven generalist teams related to a hypothetical situation; the red army from the north had met the blue army from the south in a battle of Boston. When the combat zone was finally quiet, the officers would find that the banking, educational, transportation, and other systems were in a state of disarray. The health team would discover that cholera had broken out among rats and that the nearest chlorine supply was in Worcester. When Colonel Perkins shouted the orders: "Team A will go to the State House, put the governor under arrest, and otherwise get needed information from him" and followed with similar orders to each of the other six teams, the stunned expressions on the men's faces were a study in human panic.

One amusing situation developed for which I was fully prepared. The team assigned to the secretary of education came storming into my office within an hour of their departure. In one voice they protested that that secretary did not know a damned thing about matters relating to the problem. They were right. Julius Warren had become secretary of education only two days before. Immediately I sent the men to the superintendent of the Boston schools and the priest in charge of the parochial schools, both of whom had been alerted to the possibility of a visit from our officers.

One of the graduates of our school, Colonel Charles Keegan, wrote to me from the military government headquarters in Munich, expressing appreciation for the training at Boston University. He had been appointed a military governor for Bavaria. Listening to a radio program in 1990, I was delighted to hear a woman victim of the Holocaust praise Governor Charles Keegan, who had helped her find members of her family after she was finally rescued.

The provost marshall general evaluated the programs of the ten Civil Affairs Training Schools. He gave the Boston University School the highest grade: excellent.

D. It Can't Happen Here — Or Can It?

At one of our luncheons together, Gerhard von Koshembahr, chief counselor of the German government's Department of Railroads, 1914–1933, told me this story of his ensnarement in the Nazi advance. He and his friends and associates in Berlin had scoffed at the idea of Hitler becoming more than a ridiculous nuisance in Germany's political and social unrest in the 1930s. Von Koshembahr, like most of the others, was nevertheless deeply disturbed by the economic problems; inflation was out of control and rising to astronomical heights. The Weimar Republic under Brüning, which enjoyed respect abroad, did not have the same respect at home. Rather, many deemed it ineffectual in dealing with the horrendous domestic problems.

But to people such as von Koshembahr, Hitler's outcries seemed simplistic, outlandish, and completely unacceptable. Hitler was shouting that he would defy the Treaty of Versailles; exterminate the Jews, whom he blamed for Germany's ills; and lead Germany into a millennium of *Deutschland über Alles.* How he would do all this remained a question.

Nostalgia for bold leadership in a time of crisis is an oft-repeated instinct of human beings. A danger lurks when nostalgia breeds uncritical response to the demagogue who, with dramatic flair and inflated self-confidence, calls for the masses to follow with blind trust.

So it was in the Germany of the 1930s. Von Koshembahr ended his story lamenting, "I am ashamed to tell you that I goosestepped in a Hitler parade in Berlin!"

Could it happen here?

Let eternal vigilance be the protective shield.

XII. General of the Army Dwight David Eisenhower
Pays Tribute to Daniel L. Marsh on the Occasion of the
Twentieth Anniversary of Marsh's Presidency

JANUARY 31, 1946, WAS a historically great moment in the life of Boston University. Only five months after the conclusion of World War II, Dwight David Eisenhower, general of the army and supreme commander of the Allied Expeditionary Forces, came to Boston University to pay tribute to Daniel L. Marsh on the occasion celebrating the twentieth anniversary of Marsh's presidency. Honorable Guy W. Cox, chairman of the Board of Trustees, presided and Edward C. Stone, vice-chairman of the board, was toastmaster. Anne and I were privileged to be among the thousand friends and admirers at the dinner at the Statler Hotel (the Park Plaza today).

In a fitting concluding statement to his introduction of Eisenhower, Toastmaster Stone said: "As a name that rightly stands at the very peak in American and worldwide war history, that of our guest will be indelibly written in the hearts of men. Ladies and gentlemen, I present to you General of the Army Dwight D. Eisenhower."

Stone was right. In the immediate postwar period, Eisenhower did stand at the very peak in American and worldwide war history, and however much the bricks and bats of politics would subject him to their scars, his swan song as president still should be heeded: "Beware of the dangers of the military-industrial complex."

When at last the applause quieted, the general spoke, saying (and I quote only in part): "It is an honor to come and add what I may to the acclaim that Dr. Marsh receives this evening. I go beyond giving a tribute. . . . I venture to make a suggestion to the educational world, to Dr. Marsh, and to his great University. I venture almost to challenge, why doesn't Dr. Marsh and the president of every great university throughout the world teach his people to put people of my profession permanently out of a job?" What a challenge then, what a continuing challenge today!

On that occasion, Dr. Marsh conferred upon Dwight Eisenhower the honorary degree of Doctor of Laws.

In his own opening response to the honors bestowed upon him that evening and in the presence of dignitaries from a variety of walks of life, Marsh was characteristically himself. His simple salutation was: "Mr. Toastmaster and good friends, all." He proceeded to tell us that he had approved the plan for the celebration primarily in the hope that it might contribute to the well-being of Boston University. It did. During the course of the evening, the treasurer, E. Ray Speare, presented to him a check from Marsh's friends for $100,000, to be used to complete the building fund for the new College of Liberal Arts building; and Mr. Samuel D. Saxe presented another check in the same amount from the Friends of Boston University, an organization of Jewish supporters, made in appreciation of the University's "liberal admission and educational policies." Marsh concluded his address by thanking participants (especially John S. Perkins, his assistant, for his "in-season and out-of-season service") and finally by conferring the degree upon General Eisenhower.

Nigh a half-century later, a quiver goes up and down my spine as the excitement and the meaning of that historic event again come alive in memory. Our president was being honored by the commanding general who had brought that which was only in the realm of hope in 1941 to reality in 1945: Victory!

XIII. With Lightning Speed, Marsh Names Me
Dean of Sargent College

SINCE 1941, WHEN Donald D. Durrell, Dean Davis's successor, had appointed me director of undergraduate studies and professor, I spent much of my time in the classroom. On Friday, August 4, 1945, I was teaching an early-morning course. Moments before time for adjournment, my secretary stood at the door and informed me that I must drop whatever I was doing and come immediately to Marsh's office. Dismissing the class, I said, "It sounds as if I'm about to be fired, but if I am here Monday, we shall resume our discussion."

Upon my arrival at his office, the president greeted me, saying: "You must know, George, that only a very important matter would cause me to call you from a class you were teaching." When I replied by saying that I thought that I probably was about to be fired, Marsh said, "You are going to be fired!" After a frighteningly long pause, he continued: "to take a better job." I soon found out that, in accordance with what he deemed to be his duty as it was defined by the by-laws, President Marsh, and he alone, was the "search committee" when an administrative position was open. He explained that on Thursday afternoon (of the preceding day!) he had received a communication from Nelson Walke stating that he was resigning as dean of the College of Physical Education for Women, Sargent, effective September 1. (See p. 41 for an explanation of the name of the college.) Marsh said that when that evening he had told Mrs. Marsh about the resignation, she asked, "What are you going to do now?" And she added, "You have had so many problems with that school." "I told her," Marsh said, "that, if after a good night's sleep, I feel as I do now, I shall ask George Makechnie to be dean. I do feel that way. I want you to be dean of the College of Physical Education for Women."

Lest it seem that my appointment as dean was made in panicky haste, let me remind you that the president had observed me as an assistant to the dean and registrar of the School of Education in previous years and in the two immediately preceding years as director of the undergraduate program. Do today's search committees have such an advantage?

After naming me dean of Sargent College, Marsh gave me my first assignment: to become familiar with the University's by-laws, especially Article V, sections 1 and 6, which defined the duties of the president and a dean, respectively. These by-laws, he explained, "make clear our separate duties and the administrative relationship of each of us to the other." I followed his instructions.

The by-laws made it clear that "the president is the official head of the educational system" and "director of its management" and that a dean serves "under the president's management" and "at his pleasure." At that time, the dean had a responsibility beyond supervising the educational process. The by-laws directed that "each dean shall be the custodian of the building or buildings in which his Department (school or college), or any of its students are housed."

Before, dear reader, you roll over with laughter at the thought of a college dean serving as the custodian of the building, let me relate appreciatively some of its advantages. Unrestricted by union rules until Sargent College moved from Cambridge to the Charles River Campus, our two men reported directly to me. They rendered helpful service beyond the usual functions of janitors. The senior of them, a skilled carpenter, had a small shop in the basement, where he repaired broken gymnasium equipment and other items. The other, a talented artist, prepared materials such as attractive posters for curricular and extracurricular activities. The men painted the stairs during vacation breaks and mowed the lawn in the summer. Knowing that the dean related to them as a colleague who would protect them from impossible demands of faculty members or students kept their morale high. I was deeply moved when I discovered that each of them had become a "Master Builder of Sargent Hall." Such a builder was one who contributed $150 (a large sum in the 1950s) to the fund for a new building for Sargent College on what is today the Charles River Campus.

XIV. A Wife's Honest Reaction

W HEN ANNE LEARNED of my being named dean she was less than enthusiastic. She had attended the alumni reunion in 1944 and become aware of the shocking resentment aimed at Marsh and all things Boston University caused by the deletion of the name "Sargent" from the title of the school. Morale was low. Key faculty members had resigned. When, on August 4, 1945, I told her of my morning conference with the president and his naming me dean, she responded with dead silence and finally said simply: "Do you know what you are getting into? It will take ten years off your life." During the first semester of my tenure, I thought she was right. But by the end of the second semester, a healing process had begun, especially with the students. Some old grads held their grudge for years yet to come.

The development of Sargent College and my relationship to it are extensively covered in the book *Optimal Health: The Quest — A History of Sargent College,* which President Silber commissioned me to write and for which he wrote the foreword. Accordingly, I will simply record here in these pages a few vignettes from my Sargent experience.

XV. Under Threat of Buckshot, My Deanship Begins

M Y TWENTY-SEVEN-YEAR term as dean of Sargent College began on September 1, 1945, at Sargent Camp in Peterborough, New Hampshire. In those years, the college year opened in a four-week period at the camp to prepare students to teach aquatic skills and land sports.

Two days into the session, I received a call from the chief of police. He informed me that Ben Rice, a neighbor with a large apple orchard, had registered a complaint against Sargent girls, who, he said, "already are stealing my apples."

He asked what his rights would be or not be if the next time he found them in his orchard, he fired a round of buckshot at them. The chief said, "Ben is mad as hell and you better warn your girls."

I bought a bushel of apples. After taps had been played and the campers were in their cabins, Gretchen Schuyler, a faculty member who had been a student in my classes more than a decade before, and I tied the apples to a pine tree adjacent to the main lodge, where meals were served. We posted a notice on the tree warning them of our neighbor's intent and inviting them to "steal" from the pine tree.

It worked. There were no more complaints from Ben Rice. Would a warning without apples have been as effective or would it have challenged the "culprits" to more raiding of our neighbor's orchard? At reunions, graduates of that time still tell the story of the pine apple tree.

XVI. Marsh Shows a Flair for Drama

M ANY COLLEAGUES KNEW President Marsh as an able administrator with an admirable penchant for decisiveness; few knew him as a talented entertainer with an unusual flair for memorizing poetry. The poetic droplets that he sprinkled through his otherwise prosaic pronouncements roused my curiosity. I discovered that before his coming to Boston University as president, he had given recitals of the works of James Whitcomb Riley, and using James Russell Lowell's poem

"The Present Crisis" as a text, he had given lectures on what today we might call "civil rights."

I recall that on one occasion a group of us were the Marshes' guests for dinner at what is today called "Louisa Holman Fisk House." It was Abraham Lincoln's birthday. After dinner, clapping his hands to quiet us, Marsh greeted the gathering with his usual salutation, "Good friends, all." He then reminded us that it was the birthday of the Great Liberator and he proceeded to recite from memory Lowell's "The Present Crisis," a poem of ninety lines. The following are a few lines which Marsh paused to emphasize:

> *When a deed is done for Freedom, through*
> *the broad Earth's aching breast*
> *Runs a thrill of joy prophetic, trembling*
> *on from east to west.*
>
> *Whether conscious or unconscious, yet*
> *Humanity's vast frame*
> *Through its ocean-sundered fibers feels the*
> *gush of joy or shame —*
> *In the gain or loss of one race all the rest*
> *have equal claim.*

Early in my deanship, the president accepted my invitation to give his James Whitcomb Riley recital at Sargent College. The faculty and students anticipated his coming eagerly. Members of a drama club arranged the stage with props to effect the appearance of a Hoosier kitchen. Marsh performed superbly. His Hoosier dialect was perfect. Reciting "Little Orphan Annie" with the histrionic skills of an actor, he brought screams from the audience when he shouted the lines:

> *An' the Gobble-un'll git you*
> *Ef you*
> *Don't*
> *Watch*
> *Out!*

At the close of the program, the students expressed their thanks by singing the Londonderry air "Danny Boy" with a lyric that they had written especially for the president.

TUNE: *DANNY BOY*

Oh, Danny Boy,
Now that you're here we've plans for you.
From this day on, you'll have to dress the part.
You'll sure look cute, we hope the tunic fits all right,
Our Sargent Boy, to help us in the fight.
In Modern Dance, you'll be the one to get an A;
Cut up our frogs in lab, don't let them get away.
In speech I'm sure you'd even do as well as me.
Oh, Danny Boy,
This life is misery.

Now, Danny Boy,
Please don't look blue, there's more for you.
We're glad you've come and hope you'll stay awhile.
Come on with us, take notes so we can all pass.
Our teachers dear will never cut a class.
Two hours of class
Would make a lovely day
That's just a HINT; we always dream that way.
Let's work together and be happy all the while.
Oh, Danny Boy,
You've won us with your smile. . . .

The James Whitcomb Riley recital had a beneficial effect upon the rapport between Marsh and the students and faculty of Sargent College beyond the excellence of his presentation. He had previously taken an action that grievously distressed them and the alumnae.

The controversial action took place in 1944, when Marsh persuaded the trustees to drop the word "Sargent" from the official name of the school. Please note that this was just one year before my appointment as dean. In 1945, I found that resentment fogged the school's climate. Let Marsh himself tell you why he took the action, as stated in his annual report:

At the Annual Meeting one year ago, the by-laws of the University were so amended as to give this College of Physical

Education a legal status on full equality with the other Colleges and Schools of the University. You will remember that the Sargent School of Physical Education was founded by the late Dudley A. Sargent. In 1929, Mr. Ledyard W. Sargent, Dr. Sargent's son, and Mrs. Sargent, gave the Sargent School to Boston University. In their deed of gift, they indicated that they expected the School to become a division of our School of Education. After several years of experimentation, it seemed to us that it was better to continue the Sargent School as a separate department, revising its curriculum, adding a year, and making it a regular undergraduate college in Boston University. However, in the by-laws, the name of Sargent College was perpetuated. This appeared to give it the legal status of a stepdaughter. Therefore, in order to dignify its position, and to prevent any semblance of discrimination, the by-laws were amended so as to make its style of terminology identical with that of the other departments of the University, namely: The Boston University College of Physical Education for Women.

The University is perpetuating, and will perpetuate the name of Sargent in connection with this Department of the University. In fulfillment of this purpose, the building that houses this College has been named "Sargent Hall."

All hell broke loose. The alumnae incited students to strike and otherwise protested the move. Ledyard Sargent supported the alumnae and reminded the president that the terms of the gift were intended to retain the name "Sargent" in the title of the school, not just the name of the building. Marsh and the protesters reached an agreement: the word "Sargent" might follow the official name, thus: College of Physical Education for Women, Sargent. The compromise received only lukewarm acceptance. At a luncheon of the trustees' committee on health affairs, to which I was invited because of my part in developing the program in nursing education (see p. 20), I learned how distressed some of the trustees were about the situation. They lamented that they had accepted Marsh's proposal to eliminate "Sargent" from the name of the college primarily out of their habit of voting unanimously in favor of the president's recommendations.

XVII. Marsh, the Lonely but Determined Leader

IN THE SPRING OF 1951, I learned firsthand how utterly alone during the depression years Marsh had been in his determination to relocate the schools and colleges to the new campus. Shortly before his retirement, he asked Elwood Hettrick and me to reminisce with him about his twenty-five-year term as president in an hour-long radio program on station WHDH (television was not in many homes at that time). He chose us, he said, because we had been students during his administration and he had appointed us as deans. Elwood was dean of the Law School; I, of Sargent College.

Before going on the air, we had an hour for informal preparation. Knowing that there was no age restriction on the president's term of office, I asked Marsh what had prompted him to retire at that time. He replied, "I have a sense of the meaning of symbols in life. The Scriptures say that 'the days of man are as threescore and ten years'; at my next birthday I shall become seventy. Also, I shall have served the University twenty-five years; a quarter century is a significant segment of any life."

Among other things, I asked Marsh why he unfailingly referred to the late George Dunn (who had died a short time before) as "George Dunn of blessed memory." Dunn had been a special assistant to the president, overseeing alumni affairs and like matters during the depression years, when his furniture business was less than prosperous. He was also a University trustee. With warmth in his voice, Marsh explained that the trustees, deans, faculty members, and even the treasurer, E. Ray Speare, had been giving him a hard time about raising funds for new buildings, especially those funds for a new building for the school he first proposed moving: the College of Business Administration. E. Ray, as he called the treasurer, had finally consented to accompany him to visit Ernest Howes, chairman of the executive committee of the trustees, who was wintering in Florida. After a heated discussion lasting until midnight, Howes reluctantly and half-heartedly agreed to be supportive. Remembering the event with something of a chuckle, Marsh related what happened when he and Speare returned to the hotel. He said: "I was just dozing off when there was a knock at the door. E. Ray stood there looking pale as a ghost. 'Dan,' he said, 'we can't go through with this. We have just sold the University down the river.' I said, 'E. Ray, we have made a definite decision. Go to bed and have a good night's sleep.'" The president continued. "After we had returned to Boston, George Dunn appeared in my office. 'Chief (he always called me Chief), I am with you. I'll make a supportive statement in the next meeting of the executive committee of the trustees.' He was the first trustee, or anyone else, to come to me expressing support. That is why, George, he is George Dunn of blessed memory."

The story of George Dunn was not the only one that I heard that evening before we went on the air. Marsh proceeded to tell Elwood and me the complete history of the University's move to what is now the Charles River Campus. Since we were the only two to hear it from the man himself, I find it appropriate to share it with you, dear reader:

Marsh had been adamant about the move. The College of Business Administration must be relocated on the new campus — nowhere else. As a tenant on a yearly rental basis, the school had occupied a building in the former Massachusetts Institute of Technology complex on Boylston Street, just east of Copley Square. When the restriction on the height of buildings in that area was lifted, the New England Mutual Life Insurance Company bought the property. Boston University received an eviction notice; CBA would have to move. In the depth of the Depression, the University was confronted with a critical problem. Only Marsh had the audacious conviction that anything more than a patchwork solution was possible.

Dean Lord tried to sabotage the president's effort to move CBA to the new campus. Declaring that it was "ridiculous to take a school of business out into the country," he surreptitiously looked for quarters in vacant buildings in downtown Boston. Marsh learned about Lord's actions. Perhaps the dean remembered President Lemuel Murlin's descriptive phrase when the University had purchased the land in 1920. Murlin said that the new campus site embodied "some rural charm."

Perhaps Lord also had doubts about the student-recruitment value of those three cows grazing on that land! At any rate, Marsh prevailed. At the radio-program rehearsal, he told me, "I called Dean Lord to my office. I warned him that if he persisted in his defiance of my efforts, much as I would hate to, I would not have him appointed dean the next year." (All deans were on annual appointments then. Throughout my own long deanship, I was reappointed annually.)

At the University Commencement in June 1938, Marsh announced a gift of $586,500 from the Charles Hayden Foundation. When, with beaming countenance, he literally shouted that the building for the College of Business Administration was now assured, the audience broke into thunderous applause.

The following August, Marsh, working the lever of a steam shovel, dug the first "post hole" for the first building to be erected on the Charles River Campus. Anne and I were there. It was a thrilling sight to behold. Daniel L. Marsh was "realizing the ideal" — a dream which for so long had been his north star. Only his brand of persistence could endure even when the shadows were very deep and rough seemed the course to the goal. Anne and I were witnessing one man's triumph — a triumph that would bring to reality what his predecessor, Lemuel Murlin, had envisioned and what would be a first port of entry in the University's journey toward its unification on a shared campus. The Hayden Memorial Building was completed in June 1939 and immediately occupied by the College of Business Administration.

Even the competing exigencies of World War II could not deter Marsh from his determination to raise funds for new buildings. He continued to keep trustees reminded about that need even as he responded effectively to the imperative demand for war-related programs. In 1944, the trustees authorized the executive committee to launch a drive for funds to build a new home for the College of Liberal Arts. The cornerstone for the building was laid on May 25, 1946.

The college occupied the building the following year. Other new buildings followed. The cornerstone of the School of Theology building was laid in October 1948 and of the chapel, the next year.

XVIII. The Opening in 1948 of What Is Today
the College of Communication,
and a Havana Cigar

An IMPORTANT FEATURE of the Marsh era was the annual Founders' Day convocation. Believing that an institution was strengthened by making progress in an orderly manner from its past, Marsh established the Founders' Day tradition to acquaint faculty, students, alumni, and friends with the University's past. The event was a convocation in which the deans of the schools and colleges would participate by brief readings, and the president would give an address appropriate to the occasion. Founders' Day was to come always on March 13 because that was the birthday of the first president, William Fairfield Warren.

So important did Marsh consider Founders' Day that all classes were canceled for a three-hour period. Woe unto the faculty member who did not have a convincing reason for his or her absence!

What is today the College of Communication began as a public relations school in 1947. Marsh chose the opening of the school for a Founders' Day Program in 1948. In his address at the convocation, he decried the evils of ghost writing. Among the recipients of honorary degrees, which were conferred upon a number of national celebrities in film and other communication modalities, was Skyros P. Shouras, president of Twentieth Century Fox in Hollywood.

Each recipient was asked to speak briefly at the luncheon that followed the convocation. Expressing his gratitude for the degree, Shouras said that he was proud to be a graduate of the University and that he had listened carefully to Marsh's address, which he considered to be their first lesson. He went on to remind us that that lesson was about the evils of ghost writing. He concluded by saying that he was to be the after-dinner speaker that evening. He confessed that he didn't write the speech alone. He noted that he had called upon different department heads in his organization for their contributions to it. Then came the punch line: "I hold in my hand a cigar. It is wrapped with a gold band with the inscription 'Daniel L. Marsh.' I don't think the president even smokes!" Marsh joined in the laughter. Each year he had received as a Christmas gift from a Cuban alumnus a box of high-grade Havana cigars. Thanking Shouras for his remarks, Marsh said, "True, I don't smoke, but I love the aroma of a burning cigar."

XIX. Hell Is Paved with Good Intentions: Founders' Day 1949

Following the 1948 event, Marsh asked me if in 1949 there would be anything in the history and life of Sargent College (he still said, "College of Physical Education for Women") that would be appropriate for a Founders' Day program. Gratified by his desire to honor the college, I replied that happily there would be three good reasons: 1949 would mark the one hundredth anniversary of the birth of its founder, Dudley Allen Sargent; it would mark the twentieth anniversary of the college's becoming a member of the University; and the American Association for Health, Physical Education, and Recreation, of which Dudley Sargent had been a founder and early president, would have its annual convention in Boston in April 1949.

"That's great," Marsh responded. But he added that the Founders' Day event must be held on Warren's birthday, March 13; an April date would be unacceptable. I proposed that the convocation take place on March 13, and we would invite the association to have a day-long session at Sargent College at a postponed session in April. Marsh accepted the proposal and the two programs took place as planned — the convocation in Symphony Hall in Boston and the association's meeting at Sargent College.

Marsh told me that his address would be on Dudley Allen Sargent, and he added, "You know I deplore ghost writing. I want you to get for me the names and addresses of alumnae who were at the school when Sargent was alive." He said he wanted from them only stories about Sargent, humorous and otherwise, but that they mustn't be allowed to think that they were in any way writing his speech.

The Council of Deans was strongly supportive of the event and approved our recommendations for honorary degrees to Howard Rusk, M.D., world authority on physical rehabilitation; Ruth Evans, president of the American Association of Health and Physical Education; Francisca Aquino, director of women's physical education in the Philippines; and Anna Hiss, director of women's physical education at the University of Texas in Austin (see p. 50).

Marsh's address had excellent points, but it was sprinkled with anecdotes that unintentionally set back the "healing" process once again. Responding to his request for anecdotes, some had told him that in the winter they would see elderly Dudley Sargent walking down Massachusetts Avenue holding water bottles at his sides. Both they and Marsh interpreted this as a funny mannerism, unaware that he did it to ease the pain of angina pectoris. Marsh, always lifting Boston University for praise, said that it took Sargent twice as long to earn the M.D. degree as other students at Yale, and that Yale's medical program at that time didn't hold a candle to Boston University's Medical School offering today. Marsh was unaware that Sargent carried the medical course load while he was full-time director of the Yale gymnasium. Furthermore, neither Boston University's medical program nor that of Harvard or any other institution was as high in quality in the 1870s as they had become by the 1940s.

Listening to the address, I was painfully fearful of its probable negative consequences. However well intentioned, the anecdotes, meant to be humorous illustrations, would undoubtedly be interpreted to be demeaning slurs. They were. On the following morning, Mary Russell, director of the college dormitories, came to me weeping. The students had been up all night planning protests. She said, "All the goodwill toward the University you have been building up during the last four years has gone down the drain." Soon after her visit, Professor James Wylie told me that he had dismissed his class of seniors after a period of only fifteen minutes. During that brief time, they had declared that they never again would sing the University Hymn, the words of which Marsh had written, nor would they give a penny to the building fund to move the college to the Charles River Campus.

The students also planned that Francisca Aquino would address their regular Friday-morning assembly. I knew that all the faculty and students would attend. I stayed completely out of sight during the address, and then I quietly approached the podium. Immediately there was hushed silence. Fully aware that this was a win-or-lose-all moment, I said:

> In life, often that which we anticipate with great expectation turns out to be a bitter disappointment. Such was our experience yesterday; but you must know that the University's intention and that of the president were to honor the school and its founder. Furthermore, the future of Sargent College is inexorably bound with that of Boston University. Those of you who believe me will now stand and sing the first stanza of the Boston University Hymn.

After a moment or two (it seemed to me to be an eternity) of deadly silence, the accompanist moved to the piano, then one student rose, after her a faculty member, then all were on their feet. Tears flowed freely and the hymn was sung with a feeling that I have sensed neither before nor after that critical moment.

Leaving the room, I heard the president of the senior class ask the seniors to remain. Not until graduation time did I learn that the class voted to give 5 percent of their earnings during their first five years of employment to the college's building fund, and that a Bachrach portrait of me was to be their class gift.

Later that day, I visited President Marsh. With eagerness he asked, "George, how did you like my speech on Dudley Sargent?" I told him. Whereupon he asked his secretary to bring him the note he had just received from Edgar Brightman. "Read this," Marsh said. Brightman congratulated the president on "the best Founders' Day address" he had given to date. Thus spoke the influential Brightman, and who was I to challenge his assessment? But I summoned enough courage to respond, "Doctor Marsh, I respect Edgar Brightman as an authority, if not the authority, on the philosophy of Personalism, but I question his knowledge about matters pertaining to the assignment you have given me as dean of the College of Physical Education for Women."

Then, to my delight, Marsh told me he would address the gathering of the leaders at the national convention in April and correct the false impression that his Founders' Day inadvertencies had made, and to my astonishment, he permitted me to edit his address and delete the offensive passages before it was printed in *Bostonia*.

The admission of error is a revealing sign of strength; Marsh had strength.

XX. Anna Hiss

W HEN THE UNIVERSITY COUNCIL considered my nominees for honorary degrees to be conferred at the 1949 Founders' Day convocation, some members expressed opposition to Anna Hiss. They feared that if she were honored, the worldwide negative publicity about her brother, Alger, would have a deleterious effect upon the University. Alger, who as director of the special political affairs division of the State Department had accompanied President Roosevelt to the Yalta Conference in 1945, was being accused not only of communistic leanings, but, more seriously, of collaborating with the intelligence services of the Soviet Union. Anti-communist sentiment, abetted by accusations against Hiss by Whittaker Chambers and Richard Nixon, colored the national mood. President Marsh listened to the deans who opposed the degree for Anna. Then, in firm tone, he reminded the council members that Anna Hiss was an accomplished educator with a national reputation. I recall his concluding statement: "Anna Hiss is not her brother, Alger. In her own right she deserves the degree." It was voted unanimously.

Sensitive to the University's reputation, Anna hesitated to accept the invitation to receive the degree. Only after I told her of the president's warm support and the unanimous vote of the council did she concur. In 1952, because of the continuing anti-communist crusades involving her brother, she declined to be the first president of *L'Association Internationale d'Education Physique pour les Femmes et les Jeunes Filles*.

I wrote this memoir on October 30, 1992. The morning papers carried a story quoting Russian General Dmitri A. Volkogonor, a historian with a reputation for careful research. Studying the newly opened KGB archives, he concluded, "Not a single document substantiates the allegation that Mr. A. Hiss collaborated with the intelligence services of the Soviet Union."

XXI. *Oratio ad Collectam* Delivered Solo

IN HIS BELIEF THAT the participation of the deans of the different schools and colleges in convocations such as those marking Founders' Day and Commencement would symbolize the unity of the University, Marsh had each dean read a passage from Scripture, do the invocation, or pronounce the benediction at such occasions. While these programs would be carefully planned, occasionally the human tendency to err would jar the presentation. Such an error, a printer's sin of omission, colored the Founders' Day exercise in 1950.

As was his custom, the president convened the deans the day before the event. He gave all of us our assignments. Dean Richard Conant of the School of Social Work was to lead the Collect. Marsh told him that it would be printed in the program and he should invite the audience to rise and read in unison.

While early Founders' Day programs were held in Symphony Hall and attendance was "required," by 1950, attendance had dwindled. That year the exercise was held in Hayden Hall (site today of the Tsai Performance Center). The president and deans convened for robing in a nearby room. As we left in the processional, an usher handed each of us the printed program. Richard Conant was my marching partner. Looking aghast, he turned to me and pleaded, "George, all this says is 'The Collect, Dean Richard Conant'; nothing else is printed. Do you know one?"

"Quick, write this on your program," I replied and quoted, "Almighty God, unto whom all hearts are open, all desires known, cleanse the thoughts of our hearts. . . ."

"No George, that can't be right," protested Richard. "The heart can't think!"

"You better let me finish or you'll be in trouble," I replied.

The audience stood as Richard invited them to do, but *Oratio ad Collectam* soloed by Richard Conant — even I was mum.

XXII. Marsh and I Visit the Chapel During Its Construction

ONE DAY DURING the construction of the chapel, I received a telephone call from President Marsh. He asked me to join him in front of the chapel if my schedule would permit. Even if it didn't, it did. We walked up the center aisle on wooden planks over very muddy ground. The noise was deafening. The sounds that "burst upon the ear" were not those of a "deep-laboring organ." They were the clang and bang of construction. Suddenly Marsh stopped, stretched out his arms in a characteristic pose, and above the din shouted, "George, I love the sound of construction."

How appropriate it is that the chapel bears the official name "Daniel L. Marsh Chapel." It was he who, working with the architects, planned it, and placed it literally and symbolically at the center of the campus. It was he who persuaded the City of Boston to close Ashley Street, which was between Commonwealth Avenue and the river, to become the site of the chapel. It was he who persisted, against all odds, in raising funds for campus development. The chapel, at the University's center, is a fitting monument to Daniel L. Marsh, the builder. It is also fitting that his ashes are buried there.

XXIII. Marsh "Dips into the Future": Postwar Planning

THE ORGANIZATION OF ACADEMIC departments in the College of Liberal Arts to serve also the needs of the professional schools and the activation of the long-dormant University Senate were lasting results of the work of Marsh's committee on postwar planning.

While the geographical separation of Sargent College, which was still in its Cambridge location, made it feasible to continue its academic departments, nonetheless joint appointments with the College of Liberal Arts began. Notably, Dr. Elizabeth Gardner, home-based at Sargent, became a member of the Department of Biology in the College of Liberal Arts.

Marsh consented to the reactivation of the University Senate. That body was defined by the by-laws as "the legislative body of the University in all interdepartmental academic interests which may be brought to it by the President of the University, or referred to it by the University Council." Section 9 of the by-laws stated, "The President of the University and the Deans shall constitute the University Council. It shall be the Executive Committee of the University Senate and shall have all the power of the University Senate except those which the University Senate reserves to itself."

That a "legislative body" called a "University Senate," with such comprehensive responsibilities, should have existed solely as a written description in the official Boston University Bulletin can be explained only by the prevailing campus mood here and at other institutions in that pre–World War II era. It was accepted and expected that the chief officer was exactly that: the chief. When I became dean of Sargent College and tried to involve the faculty in policy making, strange as it may seem today, they wanted me to make the decisions. Of course, Marsh made the decisions at the University level. Often a current situation in the University's affairs triggers a memory that brings with it a smile. Returning from an out-of-town meeting of university and college presidents, Marsh told me about the worry expressed by fellow presidents about the increasing demands by their faculties to be involved in institutional decisions and policy making. I recall well his reaction: "When they asked me how I was handling the situation, I told them it is a simple thing: 'I involve a faculty member when I think he can contribute something worthwhile and I don't if I think he can't.'"

With some apparent reluctance, Marsh, in due course, responded to faculty insistence (he would have preferred to call it their "suggestion") that the Senate be convened. He issued a call for a meeting of the Senate and made it clear that only he would preside.

I have a vivid memory of the final meeting of the Senate in 1951 with Marsh presiding. His retirement had been announced. Curiosity about who would be his successor was the main topic of campus gossip. Early in the meeting, Professor Sam Waxman, senior member of the entire University faculty, rose to state that in his judgment and that of his colleagues the time had come to have a representative faculty member involved in the selection process for the new president. With annoyance unmistakenly revealed in his facial expression, tone of voice, and choice of words, Marsh replied: "It is the prerogative of the trustees and of them alone," and he went on: "Any faculty member who wishes may suggest to me a name that might be considered."

Until 8:45 p.m. other business was discussed. The meeting was to adjourn at 9 p.m. As that hour approached, Waxman rose again, saying, "Mr. President." Marsh glared at Sam and muttered, "Professor Waxman." Whereupon, Sam proceeded to say that as senior member he was representing the faculties. He then read a beautiful citation of appreciation to Dr. Marsh for his outstanding leadership as president of the University for twenty-five years.

When the meeting adjourned, Marsh asked if I were in a hurry to get home or would I walk with him around the campus. Of course I agreed. It was a beautiful starlit night. Almost immediately, Marsh stopped and confessed, "George, wouldn't I have felt awful if I had further replied in anger to Sam Waxman, when he was about to read that wonderful tribute to me? I am so glad I didn't." We paused on the river side of Marsh Chapel. With deep feeling he spoke of his dream: "the raising of a replica of England's Boston Stamp." He wanted us to stand on the exact spot on which it would be located. Alas, that dream was not to be realized. Modern high-rise architecture was used to "economize" space. Thus, the School of Law building.

XXIV. Marsh Still in Command in the Year of His Retirement

ON ONE OCCASION IN 1951, an incident occurred that demonstrated that Marsh was still top boss in all matters pertaining to the University. He and I had just concluded a conference at his office in Speare Hall in the new School of Theology building, at 745 Commonwealth Avenue. We left to go together to a meeting of deans in a conference room down the road in the new College of Liberal Arts building. The ROTC unit was standing "at ease" on the sidewalk by Marsh Chapel. Most of the fellows were smoking during the interval.

As we approached the plaza, the commanding officer ordered: "Attention!" He intended to have the men turn in review formation to recognize the president. On receiving the command, the men immediately dropped their cigarette butts on the sidewalk. "Captain" Marsh took over. He clapped his hands and shouted the order: "You men pick up every one of those butts immediately." There was no "dress parade." Instead, the fellows were on their knees in embarrassed obedience.

As Marsh's first address at Boston University was to ROTC, so one of his last acts was before that same outfit. In the first instance he was the convincing orator; in the last, the commanding executive.

With the retirement of Daniel L. Marsh in 1953, a dynamic era in the history of Boston University ended even as it made possible new beginnings. The "captain" had "delivered the cargo" at the port of "unselfish service to the city, the state, the nation, and the world." In bricks and mortar, Marsh had built a new "port" — a port from which his successors could sail to greater grandeur.

By temperament and by his abilities as a leader, Daniel L. Marsh was the right president of the University for the era in which he served: 1926–1951.

Daniel Marsh, James Argeros (School of Management '51), and Harold Case (from left). Argeros was vice chairman of the Student Faculty Assembly; the president of the University was chairman.

T w o

The Harold C. Case Era

I.   The Harold-Phyllis Partnership

II.   "W'y, Rain's My Choice"

III.   A Speech, a "Suppa," and a Promise

IV.   Howard Thurman Becomes Dean of the Chapel: "In the gain or loss of one race, all the rest have equal claim."

V.   "It's the Knell That Summons Thee to Heaven or to Hell"

VI.   Howard Thurman or Martin Luther King, Jr.: Who Won the Bet?

VII.   Mrs. Thurman Seeks for the "Why" of a Student Suicide

VIII.   A Pumpkin Has Disparate Uses — Thurman Knew That

IX.   Amidst Seriousness Tempered by Levity, John F. Kennedy Receives an Honorary Degree

X.   A Subordinate Speaks Up

XI.   Lost Opportunities for Financial Aggrandizement

XII.   Dual Deanship

XIII.   "Down to Earth" — "Up in the Clouds"

XIV.   Comic Opera — The Best

XV. A Case of Mistaken Identity at the Kennedy Inauguration

XVI. "Man, She's All Yours!"

XVII. "The Play's the Thing in Which . . . "??

XVIII. Racial Equality — But Not in Our Church

XIX. The Peace Corps: The Sargent College Connection

XX. "At the Time of the Great Tragedy"

XXI. Dark Acoustical Clouds

XXII. Dual Deanships Become One

XXIII. Elephants Cast the Deciding Vote: Commencement Exercises Go to Nickerson Field

XXIV. "Time Present and Time Past Are Both Perhaps Contained in Time Future and Time Future in Time Past." T. S. Eliot

XXV. Harold C. Case Retires

T w o

The Harold C. Case Era

I. The Harold-Phyllis Partnership

IN 1951, THE TRADITION THAT a minister be president of
the University was still in vogue. Harold C. Case came to that office from
Pasadena, California, where he had been pastor of the Methodist
Church. As delegating of administrative responsibilities was something
of an anathema to Marsh, it was a natural for Case. His middle initial
"C" was for "Claude." But Treasurer E. Ray Speare kiddingly insisted
that it should stand for "Committee — Harold Committee Case."

At that time, in institutions throughout the country, faculty
demands for more involvement in university administrative as well as
academic affairs were being strongly felt. Case's style attuned easily to
the trend of the times. He appointed committees on almost everything.
Soon he added two vice presidents to his own staff: Wendell Yeo for academic affairs, Robert Oxnam for administrative affairs. Thus the Case
era began with a diminution of the authoritarian mood and the establishment of a more democratic atmosphere. Nevertheless, Case could
make his own wishes emphatically clear. He would leave no doubt that
he was the president.

More than at any previous time in the life of the University, the
president's wife played an active, albeit appropriate, role in University
affairs. Just prior to their coming to Boston, Phyllis Kirk Case had been

named 1950 Woman of the Year in Pasadena. That accolade recognized her many contributions to the betterment of the city, including her representing Pasadena at the mid-century White House Conference on Children and Youth that same year. In Boston, she continued her commitment to public service locally and nationally. She was active in the United Community Services of Metropolitan Boston, the League of Women Voters, the Urban League, and the National Association for the Advancement of Colored People.

Their daughter Rosanna's interest in drama brought the Case family and the Makechnies into early friendly relationship. In the first summer the Cases were in Boston, Rosanna became a member of the Peterborough Players, in Peterborough, New Hampshire. During the period that I was developing the comprehensive year-round program at Sargent Camp, we resided near the camp. Rosanna lived with us throughout the summer of 1951. She was seventeen years old; so also was our son Norman. Harold and Phyllis visited with us frequently. Bob Case, Rosanna's brother, came on several weekends with his friends Chris Barreca and Charlie Parrott. Throughout the ups and downs, euphemistically called "vicissitudes," of president-dean relations (sometimes less euphemistically called "squabbles"), the friendship prospered, even into the years of retirement.

The University-at-Home program, initiated by Harold and Phyllis together, was a gracious and greatly appreciated extension of hospitality to students. They were invited to the Castle, the Cases' residence, for informal discussions on timely topics with an easy give-and-take between them and their host and hostess. Each undergraduate student in the University would receive an invitation to attend at least once in his or her four-year period. The University-at-Home program received acclaim beyond the local campus. In 1959 it was awarded the Freedoms Foundation medal.

The deans had standing invitations. Often I considered the event the highlight of the week because, without calculated agenda, we engaged in animated discussion with students from a variety of cultures and from different schools and colleges of the University.

The Cases held University-at-Home sessions throughout his seventeen-year tenure as president.

II. "W'y, Rain's My Choice"

IN MY FIRST CONFERENCE with the new president, Case asked me why the college had such a clumsy name: the College of Physical Education for Women, Sargent. Explaining as best I could, I went on to point out that the name was not only clumsy, but that it was also inaccurate. Since 1932, the curriculum had included a major in physical therapy to which we now admitted male students.

Then Case astonished me with a remark that pleased me greatly, however much it might have annoyed his predecessor. He said that he had known about Sargent College and its excellent reputation even before he knew much about Boston University! He proceeded to say that he wished to visit the school, remarking that Sargent College and its young women students had a special meaning to the men of Harvard when he was a student there. In addition to official business he wanted to visit Cambridge, his old stomping ground.

We arranged a date for his visit. That morning, New England was experiencing a tropical downpour. Before Case's arrival, I gratefully recalled and recited to myself the James Whitcomb Riley lines Marsh had taught me: "When God sorts out the weather and sends the rain, W'y, rain's my choice."

During his visit, I took Case to the "upper gym," located on the top floor, with only the leaking roof above. I had placed pails to catch the streams of water, which filled containers so fast they had to be emptied while the president looked on. I recalled his parting words: "This building is obsolete. You must have a new one." A kind sentiment, but a speech and a "suppa" clinched it.

III. A Speech, a "Suppa," and a Promise

IN 1947, WITH THE APPROVAL of President Marsh, I had created a committee of students, parents, alumnae, faculty, and friends to engage with me in fundraising for a new building for the college. At that time, there was no University development office to support our efforts. We were fortunate that University Trustee Ralph Lowell, senior member of that well-known family, and his wife were unusually inter-ested in the work of Sargent College. Mrs. Lowell became chairman (it was okay to call a woman "chairman" then) of a women's committee to raise funds for the new Sargent College building.

One day I received a telephone call from Lowell, during which he asked that I give the address at the graduation ceremonies of the School of Nursing at McLean Hospital. He told me that he was president of the hospital's corporation and invited me to have "suppa" with him the eve-ning of the event. As we were eating, he thanked me for being willing to give the address and then to my astonished delight said, "As an over-seer at Harvard, I am going to ask the corporation to treat Sargent Col-lege as a friendly neighbor and buy your buildings at a generous price." He made good on his promise. The next day Lowell informed Case of his intention. The sale of our two dormitories and the college building net-ted $500,000 after the payment of $100,000 to "burn" the mortgage on Lennox Hall. Within six months, the transaction took place. With that half-million-dollar amount assured, we raised other funds from alumni and friends, including the Lowells and the Clarks. Paul Clark was presi-dent of the John Hancock Mutual Life Insurance Company and chair-man of the Executive Committee of the Trustees of Boston University. Sargent College moved to One University Road on the Charles River Campus in the summer of 1958. Opening exercises were held on Febru-ary 9, 1959.

IV. Howard Thurman Becomes Dean of the Chapel
"In the gain or loss of one race, all the rest have equal claim."
James Russell Lowell

OUTSTANDING AMONG the achievements of Harold Case was his appointment of Howard Thurman as dean of Marsh Chapel in 1953. It set a precedent: Thurman was the first black person to hold a deanship in a predominantly white university anywhere in the United States. As late as 1953, sad to say, such an appointment met racially based resistance even among some of the clergy. It took courage on the part of Case to ask the trustees to confirm Thurman's appointment — an appointment destined to break through barriers of divisiveness: religious, ethnic, and national barriers. At the time of the celebration of the University's Sesquicentennial in 1989, President John Silber declared that the appointment of Howard Thurman resounded to Case's "enduring glory and that of Boston University." Earlier, Silber had said, "The gospel that Howard Thurman preached was so universal that it breaks all barriers of divisiveness and addresses us all, whoever we are and from wherever we have come."

Howard and I were colleagues throughout his tenure, which lasted until his retirement in 1965. He was dean of the University chapel and I was dean of the University's Sargent College of Allied Health Professions. More than that, our families were friends at a level so deep that Howard and Sue became "Uncle Howard" and "Aunt Sue" to our three children, and Anne and I became "Aunt Anne" and "Uncle George" to their two daughters — a relationship which continues even beyond the grave.

Early on, Anne and I discovered that we shared a wedding anniversary date with Howard and Sue. The Thurmans were married on June 12, 1932; Anne and I, on June 12, 1933. On June 12, 1965, as one of his last acts before retirement, Howard conducted the wedding ceremony for our daughter, Joan, and son-in-law, Colin Diver. Many were the family events which the Thurmans and the Makechnies enjoyed together.

Locked in the storehouse of my most precious memories are the hours Howard and I spent alone together. We would go so far out on a promontory jutting into the Atlantic Ocean that seagulls were our only other companions. Much of our communication would be the communication of silence — active silence, creative silence, a silence that seemed to be required for the absorption of a spoken shared idea.

V. "It's the Knell That Summons Thee to Heaven or to Hell"

WHEN THE THURMANS ARRIVED on campus in 1953, as Sue observed, "For some years with fields far apart both men [Howard and I] had worked from the same agenda, to give student life (including town and gown) a rich, animated purpose, to crash stubborn walls that separate one human being from another." She added, "The two men were indeed well met." With humility, I treasure her words.

True it was, as J. Anthony Lukas noted in his book *Common Ground: A Turbulent Decade in Three American Families,* Howard and I "discovered that [we] were kindred spirits," and "before long [our] families developed a profound rapport." We also discovered that from early childhood we both had been troubled by certain doctrines of the church, in both instances the Baptist Church. At age ten, Howard listened with disbelief and distress as a minister, conducting the funeral service, "preached his non-churchgoing father to hell." Having been only eight months old at the time of my father's death, I later learned from my mother of the heaven-hell uncertainty of my father's fate. He died of typhoid fever at age thirty-one. He and my mother were "sinners" because they not only danced together but also organized a dance class on Saturday nights for married couples who enjoyed the art. Undoubtedly oversleeping accounted for absenteeism from church on many a Sunday.

Outraged and pained by the minister's fiery words, Howard murmured to himself, "One thing is sure; when I grow up, I will never have anything to do with the church." Might it be that this baffling experience temporarily detoured Howard from the ministry as his life's calling? At Morehouse College, his major was economics.

It was painful for me as a four-year-old boy to sense, even at that early age, that my widowed mother was being ill-treated by her in-laws' minister. I still recall with a touch of bitter resentment that on one occasion her in-laws' pastor ignored her completely as he shook hands with all others present in my mother's *own living room,* where she was the hostess. She had found succor in joining a group of Bible students. Their simple faith, while it extinguished the flames of hell, nevertheless troubled me because it claimed exclusive "truth" for its beliefs. "You have come into the Truth" was their greeting to new members.

Years before I actually knew him, I believed with Howard that truth "is dynamic, not static," a discovery to be continuously sought for, never entirely found; that the "ultimate" truth may be pursued down various paths; and that "all people belong to each other." It was indeed natural that we found each other to be "kindred spirits."

VI. Howard Thurman or Martin Luther King, Jr.:
Who Won the Bet?

MARTIN LUTHER KING, JR., was in his final year of resident study at Boston University when, in 1953, Howard Thurman came as dean of the chapel. The King and Thurman families had been friends since the 1920s, when Martin's father and Howard were classmates at Morehouse, and Martin's mother and Sue had met at Spelman.

Martin, Jr., was greatly moved by Thurman's preaching at Marsh Chapel. In Lewis Baldwin's book *There Is a Balm in Gilead,* Martin's Boston roommate writes: "Martin loved and respected Thurman. . . . When Thurman was speaking, he would shake his head in amazement at Thurman's deep wisdom. Thurman had a personal spiritual influence on Martin that was so lofty, and that helped him to endure." And Lerone Bennett, executive editor of *Ebony* and author of *What Manner of Man: A Biography of Martin Luther King, Jr.,* testifies that in the early days of the bus boycott, he found Martin reading "not Gandhi, but Howard Thurman" on nonviolence.

There was a close personal relationship between King and Thurman. Sue Bailey Thurman, Howard's wife, first told me of the two men's love of baseball. One day in October 1953, they both cancelled all afternoon appointments and watched the World Series in Howard's den. I have forgotten which of them cashed in on the pennies they had placed in bets!

At the reception following King's presentation of his papers to the University in 1964, I was greatly pleased to learn that he knew me better than I had thought. In the receiving line, I was about to identify myself and introduce Anne. Instead, Martin turned to his wife, Coretta, and described to her what I did in the University.

VII. Mrs. Thurman Seeks for the "Why" of a Student Suicide

Ye know the heart of a stranger, seeing
you were strangers in the land of Egypt.

SOON AFTER THEIR ARRIVAL on campus, Mrs. Thurman
became deeply concerned about the suicidal death of a Japanese student.
When she found that loneliness was a key factor, she immediately organized the International Student Hostess Committee, which consisted of
faculty and administrative wives. Anne was among them. Our lives were
enriched by the ties we made with young people from different lands.
Sunday dinner in our home was one of the delightful experiences that
supplemented those at the reception rooms established on campus.
Today, a plaque in the International Students and Scholars Office recognizes Sue Thurman as its "spiritual founder." The plaque reads:

Boston University's International Student Office
recognizes
Sue Bailey Thurman
as a spiritual founder
of the services provided to international students.
Her sensitive concern for the needs and
welfare of students from other countries
and her appreciation of the contribution
they make to the enrichment of university
life prompted her in 1953 to organize
the International Student Hostess Committee.
For three decades this group
has promoted an exchange of
friendship and understanding
between international students and
their American host families.
For her insight and foresight
we express our gratitude.
Boston University
April 9, 1983

VIII. A Pumpkin Has Disparate Uses — Thurman Knew That

An ELEMENT IN HOWARD THURMAN'S wholeness, that wholeness which he declared "must abound in all one does," was his sense of humor. His meditation "Thank God for Humor" continues to be a cheery offset to a case of the blues. "Humor," he told me many times, "is the sparkle in the water of life." Harold Case shared with me the following sparkle in Howard's personal sense of humor:

On one occasion during his tenure at Boston University, Howard was asked by President Case to attend a dinner meeting with him. On the taxi ride to the event, they commiserated one with the other. They agreed that the agenda suggested that the session would be boring and that the time would be ill spent. Nevertheless, they felt they must attend, the president having a deeper sense of that duty than did Howard. Later in the evening, on the return taxi trip, Case opined: "Well, Howard, it was pretty much the dull event we had anticipated, but that last speaker made some sense. Didn't you think so?" Howard replied, "I wouldn't know." Somewhat puzzled, the president looked at Howard, and his gaze called for an explanation. "I didn't listen to any of the speakers," Howard confessed. And he went on to say, "When the after-dinner program began, I concluded that our early negative assessment was correct, so I turned myself into a pumpkin. I could feel what it would be like to be a seed pressed down into the cool, moist earth in the spring; then, with a quickening sensation, to germinate, to feel the stirring of life, and in succession to sprout, to leaf out, to flower, to become a bud, a plant — a vegetable that grew and grew and turned golden in the fall. Just as I was going into the oven as a pumpkin pie, the chairman declared the meeting adjourned!"

Ah, yes, Howard could identify with life in its various manifestations and have fun doing it.

IX. Amidst Seriousness Tempered by Levity, John F. Kennedy Receives an Honorary Degree

JOHN F. KENNEDY, FROM the time he was a member of the United States Senate, was a supporter of Sargent College. His interest stemmed from his concern about Americans' low level of physical fitness. He knew that the promotion of health and fitness was a primary concern of the college. On one occasion he acquainted me with a couple from Australia who would be in the Boston area for two years. The husband had been named a fellow at Harvard; the wife was one of Australia's top teachers of swimming. I hired her to teach swimming. When the college moved from its seventy-seven-year location in Cambridge to the Charles River Campus in Boston, Kennedy observed in the Halls of the Senate, "Sargent College has given outstanding leadership in physical education and physical therapy . . . and now with its new building will be equipped to do an even better job."

At the Commencement in 1955, I was privileged to present John F. Kennedy for the University's degree Doctor of Laws, *honoris causa*. At that time, the exercises took place in the Boston Garden. The students marched to the platform individually to receive their diplomas. While the addresses were usually very interesting, the diploma-distribution process was tedious.

Becoming restless, Jacqueline Kennedy almost misbehaved during the long wait for the degree to be conferred upon Jack. Because of her stepmother's illness, Anne had asked our son Norman, who was a junior in the College of Liberal Arts, to represent her as Jacqueline's host. Both Jacqueline and Norman told me what happened. Jacqueline looked at her watch and timed the process. She said, "Norman, I have figured it out. We have time to slip over to Schraffts for ice cream and coffee and still get back before Jack gets the degree. Let's go." Norman replied gravely, "Mrs. Kennedy, your husband's future political fate is at stake. I think we should sit right still." It was sound advice from young lips. She heeded it. They were sitting conspicuously in the front row of a box near the stage and were objects of hundreds of curious gazes. Later, those gazes might turn into votes that would help elect John F. Kennedy president of the United States.

X. A Subordinate Speaks Up

PRESIDENT SILBER IS RIGHT in declaring that President Case's appointment of Howard Thurman as dean of the chapel resounds to Case's "enduring glory and that of the University." In 1953, it took an act of courage to nominate a black man for such a position, and it met with opposition in high places.

In 1956, the same courageous president asked me to withdraw my nomination of a candidate for a position in physical therapy because the individual was black and Catholic. His argument was that physical therapy treatment by one with such a background would be influenced negatively. I refused, saying that I found no validity in his position. There ensued a long pause in the telephone conversation, which I finally broke, saying: "Harold, in my view there are three options and they are all yours: As president you can overrule a dean, or you can support a dean, or you can get a new dean. I cannot in conscience withdraw the nomination."

Later I learned that Case made a stronger supportive statement to the trustees about the candidate than I would have made. She was appointed.

Does not a subordinate officer have a duty to oppose a position being taken by his or her superior officer on a given issue when in the subordinate's judgment that position may have unfortunate consequences?

XI. Lost Opportunities for Financial Aggrandizement

BOSTON UNIVERSITY MISSED an opportunity to greatly increase its assets when, in 1958, it turned down an offer to buy a large block of stock in the new, highly promising ITEK Corporation. ITEK was a business venture founded in 1957 by Duncan Macdonald, who was on leave of absence as dean of the Graduate School. In 1946, while chairman of the University's Physics Department, Duncan had established the Optical Research Laboratory (later renamed the "Physical Research Laboratory") for the United States Air Force. The first contract was to produce a camera capable of taking an aerial picture covering miles of surface. The camera, which weighed four thousand pounds and was the largest in the world, was completed in 1950. The University received favorable publicity when the Air Force released a clear, detailed picture of the coastal area between Boston and New York to the press. Girded by such phenomenal scientific accomplishment, Macdonald founded ITEK Corporation.

In 1958, the Air Force, which had been the principal source of support for the Physical Research Laboratory, cut its funding. ITEK promptly responded by offering to employ the personnel, rent the space, and administer the laboratory. Case turned down this offer, as well as an opportunity to buy stock, probably because (as Kathleen Kilgore points out in *Transformations: A History of Boston University*) he was "uneasy about strengthening involvement in classified military research." Case's predecessor, Marsh, had demonstrated no such uneasiness when he supported the introduction of the program in 1946. At any rate, the University forfeited highly profitable investment opportunities.

The administration also was shortsighted in not investing in real estate, particularly in the South End neighborhood of the Medical Center, when prices were at rock bottom. To no avail, Vice President Lewis Rohrbaugh and others pressed for such an investment.

Duncan Macdonald was my colleague as a dean and my neighbor as a Lexington townsman. In informal settings, he shared with me his distress that the University rejected ITEK offers. As an alumnus of the University, Class of 1940, a faculty member, and dean, he was concerned for the institution's well-being. He died in 1984 at the age of sixty-five.

XII. Dual Deanship

ON LABOR DAY WEEKEND 1959, a community-wide salute to Howard Thurman took place in San Francisco recognizing the fifteenth anniversary of his founding of the Church for the Fellowship of All Peoples — the first racially integrated church in the United States. At Howard's request, I was there for the celebration. It was a grand affair, attended by one thousand people from various walks of life.

Above. New president Harold Case speaks to students; (at his right) his daughter, Rosanna, and wife, Phyllis. March 1951.

E. Ray Speare, University treasurer; Daniel Marsh, chancellor; Harold Case, president; Atlee Percy, dean of the University (from left). 1951.

The Sargent College dance choir in Marsh Chapel. 1956.

Below. Dean George with School for the Arts students Taiko (right) and Masako Fujii, and their mother. Commencement Day. 1960.

Howard Thurman reads his piece "Deep River" at Sargent Camp. 1957.

Above. Dean George with the queen of the prom, Eleanor Keady, and her court. 1953.

The Makechnie family with Howard Thurman: Joan, Arthur, George, Norman, Anne, Howard. 1961.

George Makechnie and Harold
Case with Jean Lyman, grand-
daughter of Dudley Allen Sargent,
at opening exercises of the Sargent
College building on the Charles
River Campus. February 9, 1959.

Right. Phyllis and Harold
Case and students at a University-at-Home in the Cases'
home: the Castle. 1952.

John F. Kennedy.

To Dean Makechnie
with warm regards for four
continued success at
Sargent College. *John Kennedy*

Dean George and Dean Thurman at Sargent College. 1959.

Having dinner at home with Anne upon my return on Tuesday, I told her that the academic year 1959–1960 promised to be the easiest that I would have had in years. In the afterglow of the San Francisco experience, all seemed well with the world. Anne admonished, "I wouldn't say that if I were you; you've said so before and something has always been lurking." "But what could be lurking?" I asked as the telephone rang.

"Hello George, this is Harold, how is Anne?" came the voice of President Case, and its tone suggested something more than a concern for Anne's health. Then the "lurking" boom dropped. He told me that Robert Choate, dean of the School of Fine and Applied Arts, was in the hospital having shock treatment. He had had a complete nervous breakdown. Case said that he and Lew Rohrbaugh, the vice president for academic affairs, wanted me to be acting dean for one semester while continuing as dean of Sargent College. "Think it over and meet me at nine o'clock tomorrow morning." I replied: "You and I know that I am not schooled in art, music, or theater and will not be any more so in the morning." Because of my warm feeling for Bob Choate and the work of the school, I agreed to do my best.

Two weeks after my double deaning began, I received a communication from the president saying that he expected me "not to mark time at SFAA, but to shepherd it to its future development." In one semester! I could hardly get the sheep out of the barn in that short time, much less lead them into green pastures. Gradually the truth came out. I was to have a two-year stint — four semesters and a summer term — not one semester at what is today the School for the Arts.

The executive committee of the trustees quickly confirmed my appointment as acting dean, whereupon Vice President Rohrbaugh took me to meet the administrative staff, including the chairmen of the three divisions — Art, Music, and Theater.

Rohrbaugh had scarcely begun his introductory statement when Dr. Max Kaplan, chairman of the Art Center (which supervised community programs such as the Greater Boston Youth Symphony Orchestra), interrupted him. Clearly I recall his words: "Mr. Vice President, let me interrupt you. I know I speak for all of us here when I tell you we think that central administration has railroaded this appointment. Our assistant dean, Wilbur Fullbright, is fully competent to lead us through this crisis." The expression on every face except Wilbur's indicated that they were in complete agreement. Lew Rohrbaugh was a pipe smoker, and on that occasion the habit stood him in good stead. He knocked the ashes out of his pipe and refilled it. The activity gave him a minute or two to think of a reply to Kaplan.

Lew said, "The water has gone over the dam; the trustees have confirmed the appointment." Then, turning to me, he said, "It may be embarrassing for you, Dean Makechnie, but do you wish to speak to the group?" Sounding bolder than I felt, I replied, "Yes. I have been embarrassed before as a dean. Let me simply say that Dr. Kaplan is right in assuming that I have no expertise in art, music, or theater. But I have warm feelings for your ill dean and respect for what you and he have been doing together. Now let me be emphatic: if each of you will be as frank with me in this office as Dr. Kaplan has been, perhaps we will get along satisfactorily." Thus my two-year extremely exciting experience began.

XIII. "Down to Earth" — "Up in the Clouds"

MAX KAPLAN'S CHARGE THAT central administration had "railroaded" my appointment as acting dean of the School of Fine and Applied Arts echoed the question I, myself, had raised when President Marsh asked me to be dean of Sargent College. Implicit in Kaplan's statement was a concern that a physical educator lacked qualifications to administer a school for the arts. My question to Marsh had been that since I was not a physical educator or physical therapist, was I qualified to be dean of Sargent College, which served those two fields? Marsh's reply was that the need of Sargent College was for administrative leadership. "That," he said, "is your qualification."

Again and again, in one forum or another, friends and colleagues asked, "Don't you feel dichotomized, since Sargent College and the School of Fine and Applied Arts have so little in common?" Finally I responded by writing the following piece for *Currents,* a forerunner of the campus newspaper *Boston University Today:*

"Do you not find the School of Fine and Applied Arts very different from Sargent College?" "Is it not confusing to try concurrently to relate administratively to both?"

These are the two questions I have been asked most frequently during the last thirteen months. Usually they are followed by the observation that Sargent College seems so "down to earth" and "practical," and the School of Fine and Applied Arts, so "up in the clouds" and "impractical!"

Would the philosophers of the period of the supremacy of Athens have sensed any such disturbing ambivalence? Were not the Greeks questing the perfect harmony of body, mind, and spirit? And should not their quest be our quest today?

Through its two professions, Sargent College is concerned with helping people more fully to attain the life abundant — abundant in health and in energy, and in intellectual, emotional, social, and spiritual well being. Physical education makes its contribution by aiding in the developing of individuals strong in mind and body, buoyant in spirit, and balanced emotionally; physical therapy, by restoring to more normal health those victimized by disease, injury, or emotional conflict. The medium of physical education is positive and creative. The medium of physical therapy is positive and redemptive. Thus in its deepest dimension the work of Sargent College is that of developing the body as the temple of the living spirit.

The Arts speak a language universal and eternal, even as they are an integral part of a particular culture and a specific epoch. The School of Fine and Applied Arts provides professional training to qualified young men and women, undergraduate and graduate students, against a background of liberal education. Furthermore, it strives to do this in a climate of mutual supportiveness of Music, Art, and Theater Arts, each to the other.

The bridges between Sargent College and the School of Fine and Applied Arts are natural ones. Self-evident is the bridge of the emerging profession of music therapy as it joins dance therapy as a modality in the rehabilitation of patients.

Recreation itself is another such bridge. When recreation is conceived as ReCreation — the renewal of the spirit — the highest reaches of each of these schools are achieved.

How modern seems the Athenian point of view! The Greek idea sought the balanced harmony of the physical, the intellectual, the emotional, and the spiritual life of man. The quest for this perfect harmony of body, mind, and spirit is one of our most precious heritages. Should not intellectual and artistic activity harmonize with corresponding physical vigor? Is it not regrettable that the Greek concept of the body beautiful has not been retained with the same ubiquity as that of the building beautiful?

Who is to say that the physical educator, in striving to develop the highest perfection of the body, is not an artist of creative power and imagination? Indeed, is it not he who can provide the painter and the sculptor with their living models?

XIV. Comic Opera — The Best

SARAH CALDWELL, THAT ARTIST with genuine operatic talent — talent at the level of genius — was in the early stages of developing the Boston Opera Company when I was acting dean of the School of Fine and Applied Arts. In my first year there, she was director of the opera program.

In early December 1959, she requested that she be free of teaching duties the last two weeks of the semester to start her company on a tour through the midwest. "But Sarah," I asked, "what about your students, who will be preparing for final examinations?" With less consideration for her students than for her opera company, she tried to make a case for the value of a nationally known opera company to the school, saying that the tour would contribute to such recognition. Agreeing that a successful opera company in the community might have laboratory-like value for the students, I offered a compromise: be gone for one week, but return to classes on the Monday of the last week of the semester. Sarah agreed and assured me she would be at the school the final week.

But it was not to be so. On Sunday evening of that week, she called the assistant dean from Des Moines to say that she would not return to her classes before the end of the semester; instead she planned to take the company farther westward. When she was informed that I would not treat her absence from her students lightly at that critical time in the semester, she said she would phone in her lecture for Monday. She would have her student assistant go to station WGBH, record her lecture, then play it to her class on Monday morning. I couldn't believe what I was hearing: that she would treat students so shabbily. I was informed, "If it were not you who is dean, she wouldn't even have bothered to call."

In disbelief, I went to that class Monday morning. Sure enough, the assistant was playing the tape. He looked exhausted, having been at the radio station all night long. Sarah and Company went farther west. She did not return to her students, nor was she director of the opera program the following year. The students were delighted to have Ludwig Bergman in that post. He was a competent and conscientious authority on opera.

At this writing in September 1992, the Opera Company of Boston's most recent production was in June 1990. But Sarah Caldwell gives promise of a return to the podium. In a *Boston Sunday Globe* article, September 20, 1992, Richard Dyer notes the great successes as well as the unfortunate problems that the company has experienced since its launching in 1957. His comment had a familiar ring when he said, "In the late 1970s and early 1980s Caldwell's peripatetic prominence as America's first and foremost woman guest conductor kept her away from minding the store." This is one of the theories held by some about "what went wrong."

As in 1959 the students were not well served by an absentee teacher, so apparently in this later time the OCB is not well served by an absentee conductor. This I recognized as unfortunate, even as I agree with Andrew Porter's assessment in *The New Yorker* that Sarah Caldwell is "the single best thing in American opera."

Frequently those individuals with highly specialized skills in one area either place themselves or are placed by others in another area, where their talents do not belong. Too often the results are detrimental to the individual and to the cause in which their genius would be clearly manifest.

XV. A Case of Mistaken Identity at the Kennedy Inauguration

ANNE AND I RECEIVED the official invitation to attend all of the inaugural events in Washington, D.C. in 1960. On the day that the invitation arrived, we discovered that I had been named executor for Anne's stepmother, who had died that morning. Thus the invitation was put aside until lodging accommodations were no longer available in Washington. While Anne was not able to go, she was anxious to have our daughter, Joan, experience the event. As a high school sophomore, she was already demonstrating an interest in government. But where would we stay?

It occurred to me that Mary Rose Allen, a Sargent College graduate whom we both knew well, was a senior member of the faculty at Howard University. Responding to my request, Mary Rose said, "You come right down. Joan will be in a room with two other girls in the new dormitory, and you will be in the guest room of the men's dorm." No experience during the entire inauguration event had a more lasting and positive effect upon Joan than being the only white girl among three hundred black girls. On the drive home, she told me that she wished that her classmates in Lexington High School could be privileged to have a similar opportunity.

We were assigned to the Shoreham Hotel for the Inaugural Ball. Unlike the section in the Armory, it was delightful: a college prom atmosphere with a manageable number in attendance. Jack Kennedy and Lyndon Johnson came at 1:00 a.m. and spent a half hour with us.

We attended the Texas reception for the vice president at the Hotel Statler. Eight abreast, it took us an hour to go up the wide stairway to the mezzanine. Moving very slowly toward the receiving line, which was out of sight off the mezzanine, we were approached by a young bell-hop, who said, "Follow me quickly." He took us through a side door into a room where guests were eating, and placed us at the head of the line, with Harry Truman, Bess, and Margaret. Sam Rayburn, speaker of the house, was host. Apparently thinking we were relatives of the Trumans, who had arrived late, he greeted us, saying, "How good to see you again." Never mind that this was the first time we had ever met. Whatever else, it was a demonstration of Rayburn's well-seasoned political finesse.

XVI. "Man, She's All Yours!"

O N   A   B I T T E R L Y   C O L D   N I G H T in February 1960, our telephone rang at midnight. The voice on the phone was unmistakenly Howard's. He said in tired tones, "I know it's terribly cold, but will you come and rescue me? Susan [a student whom both Howard and I knew as an usher in Marsh Chapel] is here. She has a problem more in your field than mine. I don't know what to tell her." The night was so cold that the snow squeaked when stepped on. Weather and hour notwithstanding, duty called and I answered, driving from my house in Lexington to the Thurman residence on campus at 184 Bay State Road.

Howard greeted me at the door. He pointed to his study on the second floor and said, "She is up there. A fire is burning in the fireplace. I'm going to bed. *Man, she's all yours.*"

I found Susan whimpering. Through her tears she told me that she couldn't marry Bill, to whom she was engaged. To my question, "Why?" she responded, "Because I have a cancer of the uterus." "Has a gynecologist made that diagnosis?" "No." "Has any physician seen you?" "No." "Have you avoided seeing a doctor because you are embarrassed to do so?" "Yes." "Well, I know a gynecologist who will see you tomorrow if I request it. If I take you to her, will you go with me?" "Yes." The doctor found a functional disorder, which was readily corrected. A few months later, I attended the wedding of Bill and Susan.

"Man, she's all yours" spoke to an understanding that Howard and I had. He even said that if it might hinder the flow of a thought I was expressing by borrowing his words, I need not pause to give him credit. Of course, with deep humility I returned the privilege in matters relating to health.

XVII. "The Play's the Thing in Which . . . "??

WHEN THE MOVIE *SPARTACUS* came to Boston, the Friends of Theater, a community group that raised funds for students, took over the Savoy Theater for the opening night. They also sponsored a pre-theater buffet dinner at the Ritz Carlton. The two events combined to give the occasion appropriate glamour.

That night also marked the opening of a three-night run of the theater division's student play. That morning, Harold Ehrensperger, whom I had named acting chairman of the theater division, came to me in anguished concern. In hushed tones, he revealed the situation that was troubling him. He said, "Dean, last night a terrible thing happened. Joe [the dance instructor] rehearsed the students until they were exhausted. Finally, after midnight, he released them. They raced to the basement, and, Dean, the fellows and girls took showers together. Shall I report this to the dean of women?" "No, Harold, you have told me — that's enough. But tonight you be down there and direct traffic." "Oh, but Dean. I cannot be there; I am escorting Phyllis Case to the *Spartacus* events. Harold Case is out of town." "No, Harold," I enjoined; "You escort her to the Ritz, and after that I'll take over."

The woman who headed the Friends of Theater liked to be called "Mother Merry." In her younger days she had been an actress. That talent had not forsaken her. After dinner she said, "Aren't we having a wonderful time? Even at these tables we can raise money for the dear students. Look at the centerpieces. A friend who creates props did these wonderful papier-mâché Roman Forum pieces for me free of charge. I am going to hold an auction. How much am I offered from table one?" Whereupon Phyllis Case spoke up, "Ten dollars." "Great, great!" exclaimed Mother Merry. "The first lady of the University has started us off. What do I hear from table two?" Meanwhile, Phyllis whispered to me, "Brother, have you got ten dollars? I don't have a cent with me!"

The entrance to the theater was colorful. On the sidewalk, Lee Chrisman led the student band in martial music. Less than happy then about being a "sidewalk musician," he has long since forgiven me for assigning him a task he loathed.

XVIII. Racial Equality — But Not in Our Church

A CLASS OF 1961 SENIOR who majored in organ was director of music in a suburban church. She planned a special program to conclude her work there before her graduation, after which she would leave the area. She invited me to attend the church service on the Sunday of her finale.

The day before, a Boston University seminarian who was a student assistant to the pastor of the church had returned from the South, where he had been beaten and thrown into jail for taking blacks to "white-only" restaurants and other restricted places. He appeared at the church that morning to resume his role in the service. The pastor took every opportunity to "praise the Lord for His care of our young brother, who had done such a noble and courageous thing for the black people."

After the service, the pastor greeted the departing parishioners. To me, he said, "It is so good that you were here to enjoy your student's music program and to be part of our young brother's safe homecoming." Being familiar with the Cambridge neighborhood in which the church was located, for an aunt of mine lived there, I said, "Yes, but one thing troubles me. I didn't see a single black face in the congregation." Looking hurt, the pastor explained, "But Dean, you will understand when I say my people wouldn't stand for it."

At that time, Howard Thurman was dean of Marsh Chapel!

XIX. The Peace Corps: The Sargent College Connection

THE ESTABLISHMENT OF the Peace Corps was a notable and lasting achievement of the Kennedy presidency. I supported it enthusiastically among my students, some of whom were among the first in the nation to volunteer. Patricia Merritt, Sargent College Class of 1961, went to Tunisia and was there when Kennedy was assassinated. Knowing that she would be deeply distressed, I immediately wrote to her. She replied, saying that she was so grateful to receive my communication, because the news was garbled in Tunis. Throughout it all, she said, the image of the president's picture, which he had sent me from the White House, was constantly in her mind.

Two years before that tragedy, Kennedy had asked his brother-in-law Sargent Shriver, whom he had named director of the Peace Corps, to get in touch with me. Shriver called to ask if I would give him permission to quote me, together with Dean Paul Monroe of Harvard University, in an article he was writing for the *Journal of the National Education Association,* and which would appear on the cover of a Peace Corps brochure to be distributed among the nation's universities and colleges. Paul Monroe and I readily consented. We were pleased to receive copies of the journal and brochure. My simple contribution read, "I encourage my students to think of Peace Corps service. The Peace Corps will have a general salutary effect on education in this country."

XX. "At the Time of the Great Tragedy"

A S I W A S A B O U T T O E N T E R the Sargent College building after lunch on November 22, 1963, a Boston University police officer from across the street shouted to me, "The president has been shot!" Soon after, my wife phoned to tell me that John Kennedy was dead. It seemed the more unreal because with our daughter and her future husband, Colin, and his mother and father, we had been with Kennedy only a few weeks before, when he dedicated the Robert Frost Library at Amherst College, where Colin was a junior. Entering my office, I was saddened to be surrounded with numerous pictures of the family, which Jack's mother, Rose, had sent to me. She was scheduled to speak to a Sargent assembly the following Tuesday on the topic "Days at the Court of St. James." The pictures, additions to the presidential one I had received, were of her children at different ages. To my astonishment, just before she boarded the plane to go to Washington, Rose Kennedy called to express her regrets that she would have to cancel the Tuesday engagement.

The Sargent College/Kennedy connection was also strengthened through one Bernice Fitzgerald, who was a receptionist at the college and Rose Kennedy's sister-in-law. On that day, when news reporters confirmed that the president was dead, I took Bernice home to Dorchester, where she and her husband, Tom, were caring for his mother, grandmother to the president and his brothers and sisters. It was a sad journey, with flags being lowered and bells tolling.

A year and a half later, at Bernice's funeral, Rose Kennedy said to me, "I still regret, Dean, that I had to disappoint you *at the time of the great tragedy.*" What a great lady!

Howard Thurman, on an extended ministry from the University, was in Nigeria when Kennedy died. He was called to the American Embassy to conduct the memorial service on behalf of the United States on Sunday, November 24, 1963. Among other things, he said:

> The time and place of a man's life on earth are the time and place of his body, but the meaning and significance of his life are as vast and far-reaching as his gifts, his times, and the passionate commitment of all his powers can make it. . . . It is given but rarely to an individual the privilege of capturing the imagination of his age and thereby becoming a symbol of the hopes, aspirations, and dreams of his fellows, so that often in their enthusiasm and relief they are apt to forget that he was the symbol — that he stood for them, and his strength was their strength, and their strength was his strength, and his courage was the courage he drew in large part from his faith in them and their faith in him.

Thus the Kennedy era ended, but its significance continues.

XXI. Dark Acoustical Clouds

THE DIRECTORS OF the music programs in the School for the Arts would have been less than faithful stewards of their art if they had not tested the new acting dean in a try to get more funds than their budgets allowed. Their pleas were for worthy purposes: better public relations and the like. Each of them was a performing artist, and he or she knew right well the value of positive community responses to the public performances. The effort of one director got me into trouble, deep trouble. Happily, it finally proved to be but an interval of distress.

Allan Lannom, director of the student Choral Arts Society, came to me with the plausible case that his annual concert should take place in Boston Symphony Hall. He said that the school's concert hall was not acoustically suited to so many voices; there were over a hundred in the chorale. Several members of the Boston Symphony Orchestra were serving as adjunct members of our faculty, but that did not free us from having to pay full rent for the hall. Had I granted Allan his request, I knew that the directors of the band, glee club, and orchestra would soon be standing in line. I refused the request, but sought a way to improve the acoustics in our own concert hall.

The school was (and is) housed in the old Noyes Buick Company building, with the concert hall in the former garage. The internationally known firm of Bolt, Beranch, and Newman had installed acoustical clouds that rose in an arch over the audience seats. Bob Newman, part owner of that firm, was the father of a high school and college mate of my daughter. He and I had become well acquainted at "fathers weekends" and other social functions. I asked him to have the situation surveyed and, if alterations were in order, make appropriate recommendations. The advice was to lift the clouds over the platform to the ceiling. The cost to make the change would be $1,700.

I convened the directors: Allan Lannom; Lee Chrisman, band; Marvin Rabin, orchestra; James Houghton, glee club; and Richard Joachim, performance coordinator. Unanimously, they agreed that I should request the extra money needed to proceed with the alteration. I made the request of Treasurer Kurt Hertzfeld, pointing out the permanent saving that such an expenditure would make over repeated rental of Symphony Hall. He readily approved: the clouds were lifted.

The chorale's concert went beautifully. Except for a lack of enthusiasm for the less-attractive-to-the-eye new cloud formation, everyone was pleased. The quality of the music was excellent.

The next week the annual band concert took place. The lifted clouds in no way lifted the spirits of the players, much less those of conductor Lee Chrisman. What had been acoustically good for the chorale was horribly bad for the band. The sounds did not qualify to be called a concert. Lee bounded into my office the next morning. Although he was one of those directors who had approved the new cloud formation, he had found it to be threateningly dark the evening before. He surely was faithful that morning to my first request when Lew Rohrbaugh introduced me in September. Lee was giving it to me with a vengeance "right in my office."

I returned to the treasurer. "I have come to talk about the acoustical clouds, Kirk, that you allowed me $1,700 to raise."

"How did it go?" he asked.

"It was the worst damn mistake I ever made as a dean." I replied. "I need the same amount to get them down again."

In his silence he seemed to say "Incredible!" Then he replied, "You are the first dean who has ever confessed to me that he made a mistake. You have the money to lower the clouds. Get them down."

How good it is that today in retirement, Lee Chrisman continues to conduct the Alumni Concert Band. Out of loyalty, warmth, and respect for him, the members come from distant places to play at the Commencement ceremony and at other times throughout the years. I delight in attending these truly exciting Alumni Band concerts.

I hear you asking, dear reader, "What happened to the Choral Arts Society's annual event the following year with no Symphony Hall available and no raised acoustical clouds?" The event was a successful concert which received much applause. The conductor had made a good, if not somewhat expensive, try for Symphony Hall, though.

XXII. Dual Deanships Become One

MANY INDIVIDUALS' RÉSUMÉS were considered by President Case, Vice President Rohrbaugh, and others as they "searched" for a permanent SFA dean. At Rohrbaugh's request, my name was on the list, and it was still there when the many became two: Edwin Stein and myself. After careful consideration, I informed Case that I wished to return to Sargent College full time to develop the allied health professions programs.

I had thoroughly enjoyed the two years with the artists, students, and faculty of the visual arts, music, and theater. It was indeed a new experience, increasing my appreciation of the arts. My "shepherding of the school toward its future" consisted primarily of securing new leadership in music and theater. I was grateful for the goodwill extended to me by students as well as faculty, and especially for the written assessment that Max Kaplan, who had been so forthrightly opposed to my appointment, made to the president. Dr. Kaplan moved that the executive committee formally voice appreciation. His motion said in part:

> It is the unanimous desire of the Faculty of the School of Fine and Applied Arts, through its Executive Committee meeting, to express its deep appreciation to Dean Makechnie for his untiring effort in time, energy, and thought during the past two years.
>
> Without professional background in the highly specialized and complex activities of music, theater, or art — yet with a keen awareness of their significance within the University and the American culture — Dean Makechnie displayed an ability to absorb their complexities in administration quickly and with a keenness of perception which enabled him to come directly to the heart of our needs and concerns.

Ed Stein had come to the school from having been dean of music at the University of New Mexico. He was well received by the faculty and students and proved to be a successful dean.

XXIII. Elephants Cast the Deciding Vote: Commencement Exercises Go to Nickerson Field

BEFORE 1928, THE UNIVERSITY had no outdoor facilities for recreation and sports. That year, funded by a gift by William E.

Nickerson, an officer of the Gillette Company, Nickerson Field in Weston was dedicated. The band played, and President Marsh and Mr. Nickerson led the rest of us in a parade up and down, around and across the acreage. The combination of grassy field surrounded by woods and bordered by the Charles River made the site a delightful place for athletic games, tennis, canoeing, and, ah yes, courting. Anne and I went there frequently. Marsh enjoyed presiding at alumni reunions there.

Often on Saturday afternoons, Edgar Brightman and I would sit together on the train, which took us from the Back Bay Station to Riverside in Weston. Today the site is where the Massachusetts Turnpike and Route 128 and U.S. 95 intersect. No, Brightman and I didn't discuss the philosophy of Personalism (of which he was the leading exponent); rather we lay non-monetary bets, we called them "figuratives," on the outcome of the forthcoming football game. Win or lose, we always won. Whatever the scoreboard might have recorded to the contrary, E. Ray Speare, the treasurer and a former B.U. football player, would righteously proclaim "Victory." Of course "a Methodist moral victory. Does not Scripture entreat us to 'love our enemies' and do good to them?"

By happy timing the sale, by eminent domain, of Nickerson Field in Weston for the construction of the turnpike came coincidentally with the departure of the Boston Braves baseball team from Boston. The University bought Braves' Field and changed the name, appropriately, to Nickerson Field.

Boston University Commencements had always been held indoors. By the 1960s, the increased attendance made the facilities at the Boston Garden less desirable. President Case dubiously toyed with the idea of an outdoor Commencement at the new Nickerson Field. But he wondered, what if it should rain? He asked Treasurer Hertzfeld to check with the United States Weather Bureau about weather conditions on the first Sunday in June over the previous ten years. He found what any farmer already knew: Sometimes it rained, often it was fair, and even more often it was threatening. While Harold was pondering, by chance I was with him at a social function when James Conant, president of Harvard, joined us in informal conversation. Harold asked, "Jim, I know that Harvard's commencement is traditionally outdoors. What do you do if it rains?" Conant's reply was Harvardian and simple, "God wouldn't dare!" Even that otherworldly assurance did not convince Harold. He was a clergyman and knew right well what the Book said: The rain falls "on the just and the unjust."

While the president of Harvard could not convince Harold to take Commencement outdoors, elephants did. The 1961 exercises came on Sunday, June 3. The Barnum & Bailey Circus had performed at the Garden the previous week. They finished on Saturday, June 2, and vacated the building after midnight. Our platform party marched the next day where the elephants had just been. Thoughtfully (or was it naturally?), the good animals had left us souvenirs generously spattered over the floor!

The 1962 Commencement was held at Nickerson Field.

XXIV. "Time Present and Time Past
Are Both Perhaps Contained in Time Future
and Time Future in Time Past"

T. S. Eliot

My TWO-YEAR DUAL DEANSHIP, with its time demands, had put on hold the transformation of Sargent College as a school serving only the physical education and physical therapy professions to one centrally involved in the development of a timely new concept: the allied health professions.

The phenomenal increase in the first half of the twentieth century of scientific knowledge, particularly of health science, demanded new health specialties. At the beginning of the century, the triumvirate of medicine, nursing, and dentistry sufficed to provide health care, and each was a unit in itself, i.e., without special subdivisions. By mid-century, there were twenty specialties within the nursing professions alone, ranging from nurse anesthetist to public health nurse. Each specialty requires its own skills and personal temperament: the nurse anesthetist serves patients in a hospital when they are unconscious; the public health nurse serves in a private home, where a grandmother from the "old country" may be protesting violently a new treatment that she considers to be at odds with old mores, perhaps even at odds with religious traditions.

By mid-century, Sargent College needed to adapt its program to new knowledge that had evolved from Dudley Allen Sargent's early concepts. A medical doctor a century ahead of his time, Sargent practiced "preventive" medicine. "I felt," he said, "that I had seen a gleam that I must follow, and that gleam was preventive medicine. . . . I hurled myself at the goblin, disease, from that unconventional angle." He suffered the taunts of fellow physicians who thought the treatment of disease was the only worthy commitment of a doctor. He also suffered personally the lack of the high financial compensation his colleagues enjoyed. The physical training program that he had developed "to fortify the well, give strength to the feeble, and hope to the despondent" contained in embryo the health specialties that would develop by mid-century. My return on a full-time schedule to Sargent College helped give impetus to that development.

In 1957, while the college was still located in Cambridge, President Case and the trustees approved our request that occupational therapy be added. To commemorate the move to the Charles River Campus, with expert assistance from Emmanuel Goldberg, director of University public relations, and in collaboration with our medical advisory committee and faculty, we produced a written symposium addressed to the topic "Do Americans Have Sufficient Health and Energy in the Modern Era?" The symposium triggered editorials in newspapers throughout the country. *The Boston Traveler* and *The New York Times* gave it multi-column news coverage. Acclaiming its timeliness, Sara M. Jordan, M.D., co-founder of the Lahey Clinic, based one of her nationally syndicated columns on the symposium's theme. It also triggered an editorial in *The New England Journal of Medicine,* which, recalling the nineteenth-century origin of the school, hailed Dr. Sargent as "a pioneer in the appraisal of the human machine, especially in terms of muscular development and its effectiveness in terms of . . . work capacity." In the *Congressional Record,* January 20, 1959, Congressman Thomas J. Lane commented on the school's long service to physical education and physical therapy, and included one of the symposium's articles with his remarks.

XXV. Harold C. Case Retires

CASE CONCLUDED HIS sixteen-year term as president when he reached the new mandatory retirement age of sixty-five, in 1967. In accordance with his style of delegating responsibility to deans, he had appointed vice presidents for the first time in the University's history. During his tenure, the University moved markedly from its primarily local enrollment to a national and international student body. This change brought a demand for housing. Between 1963 and 1965, Claflin, Rich, and Sleeper Halls were built in an arc bordering Nickerson Field's playing area. Warren Towers, named for William Fairfield Warren, William M. Warren, and Shields Warren, opened at 700 Commonwealth Avenue. Recognizing ethnic and religious diversity on the campus, Case appointed Howard Thurman as dean of the chapel and approved Catholic services. The first mass was celebrated in October 1952. The new Hillel House opened in 1953.

By action of the trustees, the athletic center at Nickerson Field bears Case's name. The selection of the athletic center as a memorial was interesting, as President Case was at one point at odds with athletics, specifically football. Earlier in his term in office, he had proposed to the Deans' Council that football be eliminated at Boston University. His proposal, which was approved by the Deans' Council, was based on a concern that athletic programs at that time tended to compromise a university's dedication to high academic standards. Needless to say, Case's efforts were met with vigorous opposition by certain alumni and the football schedule remained the same. Is there not a bit of irony, then, that the facility is called the Harold C. Case Athletic Center?

Dean George Makechnie; Virginia Apgar, M.D., creator of the Apgar Test to determine the condition of infants seconds after birth; Mildred Elson (Sargent College '21), first president of the World Confederation for Physical Therapy; President Arland Christ-Janer. 1969.

The Christ-Janer Years

I. A Long Tradition Is Broken: A Non-Methodist Minister Becomes President — Arland F. Christ-Janer

II. Sargent College of Allied Health Professions Conducts First Nationwide Conference Teaming Occupational Therapists and Physical Therapists

III. The Charter Centennial Becomes a Series of School and College Events; Graduate Programs

IV. "To Be or Not to Be" — That's the Commencement

V. Too Many Women on Campus — No Way!

VI. "The Bombs Bursting in Air"

The Christ-Janer Years

I. A Long Tradition Is Broken:
A Non-Methodist Minister Becomes President —
Arland F. Christ-Janer

ARLAND F. CHRIST-JANER succeeded Harold Case as president of Boston University. From his inaugural convocation in October 1967, he demonstrated an informal style. For example, to the embarrassment of a president's host, he asked that his inaugural speech be interrupted when Red Sox scores were made so that he could announce them to the audience. Faculty members were less than favorably impressed with such a departure from tradition.

Christ-Janer came to the University from having been president of Cornell College, a Methodist institution in Iowa. He was not a minister; thus he broke the tradition that went back to the founding that a Methodist clergyman be president of the University. A graduate of Carleton College, where he majored in philosophy and Greek, he had also earned degrees in the Yale School of Divinity and the Chicago Law School. His hobbies were golf, swimming, and painting. His paintings, in modern motif, were well received. A one-man show in New York earned favorable reviews.

Arland created a more relaxed social atmosphere on campus with libation — moderate libation — succeeding abstinence — total abstinence.

Such a change was not announced as official policy. He would not indulge in drinking "when it is likely to be offensive to some," but he acknowledged that he enjoyed a nip of scotch or a draft of beer with "spaghetti" and, who knows, perhaps with other delicacies.

The Christ-Janers preferred to live off-campus rather than in the Castle. Perhaps he foresaw the student uprisings that were to characterize campus life throughout the nation in the late 1960s.

The more relaxed ambiance was generally welcomed. The stricter policy in relation to alcohol had engendered a measure of hypocrisy. In 1963, I determined that the veil of hypocrisy must be lifted at the Sargent College senior banquet the following year. At the 1963 event, students had gathered in the restaurant's lounge for cocktails in the hour before the banquet. For the same libation, faculty had gone to lounges in other places. At a half minute before dinner was served, the faculty arrived. Each group knew full well where the other had been!

Two weeks before the 1964 senior banquet, while Case was still president, I had a conference with Margaret Merry, executive assistant to President Harold Case. Opening the conversation, I said, "Margaret, I have come to inform the president's office of an invitation Anne and I have sent to members of the faculty. It asks them to join us and the seniors at six o'clock in the lounge of the Sonesta Hotel to enjoy fellowship together in the manner that a lounge atmosphere provides. At seven o'clock we will all go into the banquet hall and only water, tea, and coffee will be served. I have come for neither approval nor disapproval, only to inform the president's office of the plan." Margaret was laughing heartily as I departed.

The senior banquet was on a Thursday evening. The following Monday I was attended by Gus Harrar, director of the Mugar Library, and Jack Fielden, dean of the College of Business Administration. Gus had served sherry at a meeting of the Friends of the Library and Jack had served beer at an alumni gathering in Gloucester. Both had been "called on the carpet" by Case, and "given hell" for their action. They asked me "how in hell" had I gotten away with having even spirits served at a senior banquet? Answer: "I informed the president's office of my deviltry."

II. Sargent College of Allied Health Professions
Conducts First Nationwide Conference
Teaming Occupational Therapists and Physical Therapists

SARGENT COLLEGE WAS the first in the nation to offer programs in the allied health professions with a curricular range from the freshman year through the doctoral years. That such comprehensive programs made teamed learning and teaching possible attracted the attention of national leaders.

In 1966, Clara M. Arrington, physical therapy consultant in the Department of Health, Education, and Welfare's (HEW) Children's Bureau, and Wilma West, occupational therapy consultant in the same bureau, proposed that the college conduct a week-long symposium on chest disorders in children, which the bureau would finance. Funds would provide tuition, travel, and living expenses for the occupational therapists and physical therapists whose applications were accepted, honoraria for faculty, and publication of the seminar's proceedings.

The college presented the seminar in March 1967. Therapists from institutions throughout the country that had established or saw the possibility of establishing treatment programs for children with chest disorders were welcomed. The chairmen gave preference to practicing therapists who applied as teams to represent their institutions and to faculty members in colleges and universities where the curricula included the theory and principles of therapeutic treatment of children. One hundred occupational and physical therapists enrolled. In addition, the college invited occupational and physical therapy students and those in other nearby schools to attend the lectures and demonstrations. For the first time at the national level, occupational therapists and physical therapists were brought together to deal with a common problem.

The faculty comprised twenty-one recognized specialists: professors, practitioners, and researchers in anatomy, physiology, psychology, medicine, social work, occupational therapy, and physical therapy. The seminar covered "normal respiratory and cardiac structure and function; [and] alterations in structure and function produced by chest problems . . . potentially amenable to treatment by occupational therapy and physical therapy." The proceedings were widely distributed. Under a contractual arrangement between Boston University and *Physical Therapy,* journal of the American Physical Therapy Association, symposium papers were published in the May, June, and July 1968 issues of *Physical Therapy* and in a monograph, *Chest Disorders in Children.*

A rewarding spin-off: In consultation with Clara Arrington and Wilma West, I presented a proposal for a follow-up program, which HEW subsequently funded.

III. The Charter Centennial Becomes a Series of School and College Events Graduate Programs

PRESIDENT CHRIST-JANER chose to recognize the University's Charter Centennial in 1969 with a series of programs conducted by the individual schools and colleges. Coming at the time of its transformation, the plan was especially opportune for Sargent College as it moved from being an undergraduate college exclusively, to include a graduate school with accompanying new offerings in the health professions. Each school and college was provided with a special budget for its centennial presentation.

As in 1966, when funds provided by the United States Department of Health, Education, and Welfare enabled us to present a program that garnered national recognition for its quality, so the funds provided by the University for the Centennial gave us a similar opportunity. In 1969 Mary Switzer, then administrator of the Social and Rehabilitation Services Administration, Department of Health, Education, and Welfare, was with us. Speaking at a luncheon session, she observed that unlike the programs of some hastily organized schools of allied health that had "jumped on the band wagon" to get funding through the Allied Health Profession Act of 1966, the Sargent College program represented "an orderly development from its beginning." In a private conference, she told me of her enthusiastic approval of what we were developing and assured me of her continuing support. By my retirement in 1972, that support was represented by $1,000,000 plus.

At a convocation climaxing our celebration, honorary doctoral degrees were conferred upon two outstanding leaders in the health professions: Virginia Apgar and Mildred O. Elson. Virginia Apgar, M.D., was the creator of the "Apgar Scale," by which the physical condition of babies is measured minutes after birth. Virginia had participated in a day-long program the college offered, in cooperation with the March of Dimes Birth Defects Foundation, for high school seniors. The program was entitled "Youth Conference on Birth Defects." Over one thousand students from throughout New England attended.

Mildred O. Elson, the other degree recipient, was a graduate of Sargent College in 1921, the first physical therapist to use the Hubbard Tub in the treatment of poliomyelitis, the first executive director of the American Physical Therapy Association, and the first president of the World Confederation for Physical Therapy. Mildred contributed greatly to the college's transformation. I treasured her counsel as a consultant to me.

IV. "To Be or Not to Be" — That's the Commencement

IN 1970 CHRIST-JANER appointed me chairman of a committee to devise a new format for the Commencement ceremony and to suggest a speaker for the forthcoming event. Other members were a trustee, a faculty member, two students, and James Baker, vice president for public affairs, ex-officio. Gertrude Clapp, my long-time assistant, served as secretary. Provoked by negative reactions to the war in Vietnam, campus unrest marked the year. Student members of such committees were chosen to include at least one of the student "rebels," who didn't "trust anybody over thirty." Usually such a student flashed a bandana and a red headband.

Having been appointed in late February, the committee experienced difficulties in securing a speaker. While the students' recommendations were excellent, their choices (people such as John Gardner, secretary of the Department of Health, Education, and Welfare, and Archibald MacLeish, distinguished author and librarian of Congress,

BOSTON UNIVERSITY
Currents
INCORPORATING THE WEEKLY CALENDAR

Vol. 2, No. 27   May 7, 1970

COMMENCEMENT OFF, GRAD SCHOOLS NORMAL

All Undergrad Exams Canceled

BU ON STRIKE brought this crowd of students together Tuesday for a sit-down on Bay State Road, before they marched to the State House for an all-college protest demonstration.

Boston University, hit by strike action, has canceled all final exams and Commencement exercises for its undergraduates. More than 17,000 students are affected.

The step was taken by the University Council late Tuesday after a long meeting on issues and events related to the strike situation. The statement announcing the action pointed out that the decision was concerned with "the personal security of students."

The full announcement of the unprecedented step reads:

"The University Council, at a meeting this afternoon with student leaders, passed the following resolution:

"The University Council views with grave concern the fact that in our society, an institution of higher learning must be forced to consider the interruption of the academic process. Nevertheless, the massive expression of student

(Continued on Page 8)

BU to Mail Grades, Hold Summer School

The Office of Academic Affairs, in a statement issued yesterday, set forth University plans to deal with undergraduate departures and to conduct normal Summer School registration.

The statement said:

"The cancellation of undergraduate examinations and the closing of

dormitories by 5 p.m. Thursday was decided by the University Council in consultation with faculty representatives, Student Union leaders and many of the college and school student presidents.

"It was agreed that a clear and present danger to personal security exists on campus, particularly in the

large residence halls. Again last night there was vandalism and false fire alarms. Bomb scares have occurred today. Fire damage to the Administration Building amounts to over $5,000.

"No academic penalty will be incurred by undergraduates due to the cancellation of the

remaining five days of examinations.

"Grades will be mailed to all undergraduates and diplomas will be mailed to seniors.

"All outstanding balances should be settled with the Bursar's Office immediately. Reimbursement of deposits for caps and gowns will be made.

Refunds for caps and gowns can be obtained at the Book Store.

"University offices will remain open and faculty will be on hand. Summertime registration will begin as scheduled tomorrow and Friday in Sargent Gym and will continue May 18 to 22 at the Summer School Office."

OFFICE GUTTED BY FLAMES

Molotov Bombs Start Fires

Fires struck varied campus targets Monday night and early Tuesday morning – the Administration Building at 147 Bay State Road, the Astroturf at Nickerson Field, the School of Fine and Applied Arts, and an incinerator area in a Bay State Road dormitory.

Campus police were kept busy in the early morning hours. Bomb scares and fire alarms also brought response from the Boston Fire Department more than a dozen times.

In the Administration Building, the office of Ann Peterson, assistant to Senior Vice President Everett Walters, was burned out when

a fire bomb was hurled into the building from the back, causing damage estimated at $5,000. Walters' office was charred.

The Administration Building fire, occurring at 3:50 a.m., was followed moments later by a fire at the School of Fine and Applied Arts. The SFAA blaze, caused by a fire bomb, resulted in water damage to a theater rehearsal room.

At 4:25 a.m., fire was reported on the Astroturf, and a patch the size of a desk top was burned. At 5:10 a.m., fire was discovered in a dumpster at the rear of the Law-Education complex.

Fire alarms were also sounded at 167 Bay State Road, West Campus 1 and 3, Charlesgate and 700 Commonwealth Avenue. There was a bomb scare at Mugar Library.

Police were also called for students trying to break into Myles Dormitory, and for students fire-bombing along Bay State Road at 3:25 a.m. Windows were broken at 125 Bay State Road at 5 a.m.

Throughout the day, fire trucks were stationed in the area of 700 Commonwealth as a precaution and for swift access to the campus if necessary.

FIRE-BOMBING touched off the flames that wrecked this room in the Administration Building — the office of Ann Peterson, assistant to Vice President Everett Walters.

1939–1944) were unavailable. Their speaking engagements had been booked for months. The committee had considered Senator Ted Kennedy, but rejected him in favor of Senator Claiborne Pell. On receiving the committee's recommendation, Christ-Janer invited Pell to give the Commencement address and to receive an honorary degree. Pell accepted the invitation. Shortly thereafter, Pell and Kennedy chanced to meet in a senate lounge. During their conversation, Pell told Kennedy that he was giving the address at Boston University. A surprised Kennedy retorted, "I thought I was to be the B.U. Commencement speaker this year."

Sensitive to Kennedy's priority-claim on Boston turf, Pell informed Christ-Janer that, under the circumstances, he felt compelled to recall his acceptance of the invitation. Facing the dilemma, the president dispatched Baker to "tell George." Baker told me that to their dismay, the president's office had discovered that the chairman of the Board of Trustees, without notifying Christ-Janer, had invited Kennedy to give the address. In panicky tones, Baker asked, "What shall we do? How will the students react?" "You arrange with food services for a breakfast in the Estin Room at eight o'clock tomorrow morning," I replied. "We'll have a meeting of the committee there." One of life's ironies: The Estin Room is named for the father of the then-chairman of the Board of Trustees.

The meeting went well. When the members of the committee sensed the president's problem, they expressed their support of him. Looking straight at a student "rebel," I called for a vote. He was the one who moved that the committee recommend the substitution of Kennedy for Pell. The members concurred unanimously.

Our other assignment: to recommend a change in the format for the ceremonies. A single ceremony with a speech and the conferring of several thousand degrees, including the distribution of diplomas, had become unwieldy. The committee recommended that the speech and the act of conferring degrees be done at the ceremony at Nickerson Field, but that the distribution of diplomas take place in separate ceremonies for each school and college. The new format now allows for a more congenial setting for parents and friends.

But alas, the first Commencement under the new plan didn't take place. Bomb threats made it inadvisable to hold Commencement at the field. A fire bomb thrown into the president's office building at 147 Bay State Road had done serious damage, especially to one of the beautiful carved doors. The general mood on campus was tense. A simple ceremony was held in what is today called "the small ballroom" in the George Sherman Union building. Kennedy spoke to a small audience. Only honorary degrees were conferred there; the students received their diplomas by mail. I held a private ceremony for a student from Germany and her family (who had flown in for the occasion) in my office. The president approved my conferring the degree.

A sequel to the committee experience: In 1974, Anne and I flew out to Chicago where, in a family service, Howard Thurman dedicated our grandson Brendaen to God. At the airport for our return flight, we met the rebel-student member of the committee that had worked in that uncertain atmosphere those years before. He was now an officer of American Airlines. After a pleasant chat with him, we boarded the plane and took our seats in the tourist section. Before take-off, we were approached by an officer, who told us that our young friend wished us to travel first class back to Boston as guests of American Airlines. "The contradictions of life are not final" was Howard Thurman's discerning insight. How true!

V. Too Many Women on Campus — No Way!

ON ONE OCCASION, Christ-Janer called a two-day meeting of the University Council. Toward the end of the first morning session, Jack Fielden, dean of the College of Business Administration, scathingly denounced the trend toward more women, students and others, in the University community. His argument was that such a trend would be detrimental to fundraising because a husband traditionally would make a larger contribution to his alma mater than a wife would to hers, and single women were not generous givers. The irony of the charge was that, under pressure from the University community, the president had just recently returned a naming gift of $500,000 to a donor whose business reputation was suspect, and the Women's Council then replaced the amount.

I raised my hand to speak. The presiding officer, Vice President Everett Walters, said, "No, George, we are about to break for lunch." I protested, "If you don't let me say one-minute's worth, I'll get indigestion at lunch." With a frown, Walters yielded. I said, "For the last several years, the University has received an average of $70,000 annually from the HEW's Office of Rehabilitation. I remind you that it would require a large endowment to produce that much income. We negotiate with and receive final approval from administrator Mary Switzer, who is a woman. That's all I want to say."

A few days later, I sent the following letter to Christ-Janer. I learned from Gladys Hardy, his assistant, that he shared my communication with his entire staff. The recommendation in the postscript was approved by him and the trustees.

> The purpose of this communication is simply to share informally with you some observations that I have made over a forty-year period, particularly relating to the position of women in Boston University.
>
> Some of the discussion at our recent and very effective two-day council meeting seems to keep creeping back into my mind, causing a slight uneasiness. It was evident that a number of colleagues were disturbed about what appears to be a trend that more women are enrolling as students in the University, and that, for various reasons, this in turn might adversely affect fund-raising as we move into the second century.
>
> While recognizing the desirability for an enrollment reasonably well balanced between the sexes, I do not share any deep sense of disturbance about the present apparent trend. Sargent College and the School of Nursing in their development have naturally contributed to an increase in the number of women students in Boston University. For our part, we are seeking, not to reduce the number of women students, but rather to increase the number of men attracted to the allied health professions. We are doing this not alone

because such a balance may be better for Boston University, but that it is also desirable for the professions themselves. My uneasiness relates less to the fact that an increasing number of women students are enrolling in the University, and more to the fact that so few women, over the years, have occupied decision-making positions in the University. My experience indicates that when women are in positions of decisive leadership, they themselves seek a balance between the sexes in such matters as student enrollment, professional appointments, officials elected for national organizations, and the like. The recent appointment of Royce Noland as executive director of the American Physical Therapy Association is a case in point. The Board of Directors of the Association are predominantly women, as is the Association itself, which has elected Eugene Michals as its president.

Also, there is evidence that the position of women in the life of our society is changing. In 1963, under the authorship of Betty Friedan, the book entitled *The Feminine Mystique* was published. Though not scholarly, it is suggestive of a trend indicating that women are seeking for their own sense of fulfillment gainful and equal employment in the professions and in other vocations. I am convinced that this trend is very real, and that society and its institutions will be the richer because of it.

Only yesterday Shields Warren and I were talking about the magnificent contribution which Mary Switzer made as an outstanding woman in government. My own acquaintance with her began in the 1950s, when she was the director of the Vocational Rehabilitation Administration of the Department of Health, Education, and Welfare. I have watched her grow in stature as a national and international leader. As you know, she is now the administrator of the Social and Rehabilitation Service. The first grants from this source were authorized in 1955. For the academic year 1955–56, the University received $69,119.80. By 1957–58, this had been increased to an amount of $122,242; and last year,

1968–69, Boston University received $750,000 in grant support through her office, under its various names.

Though the number of women officials — academic or administrative — who have been involved in the history of Boston University have been relatively few, their influence and contribution, nevertheless, have been highly significant.

A few "for-instances":

The School of Medicine was established in 1872 at Boston University by a merger with the New England Female Medical College which, in turn, had been founded in 1848 as the first medical college for women in the world.

And was not Rebecca Lee, a graduate of the school, the first Negro woman in the United States to receive a medical degree?

From my personal knowledge, the late Elise Nelsen was persuasive in convincing Ledyard Sargent to tender Sargent College and its buildings to the University in 1929. The sale of these buildings and the dormitory to Harvard University in 1958 netted approximately a half million dollars, which was applied to the cost of our relocation on the Charles River Campus.

The first dormitory built by the University as a women's residence was Lennox Hall, on Massachusetts Avenue in Cambridge. This was opened in 1931 to house the students of Sargent College. The financial genius of the then dean of women, Lucy Jenkins Franklin, made this possible. Somehow she persuaded bankers to give what amounted to about a 100% mortgage that was paid off over the years by income to the dormitory. As indicated above, the proceeds from the sale of that building to Harvard eleven years ago made a substantial difference when we were relocated in our present facilities.

In the late 30s when, if there were a central campus, it was in the Copley Square area, and we just did not have facilities that would lend grace to important social occasions. Even for the smallest dinner party, a hotel room had to be hired. It was then that the Women's Council presented the building at 146 Commonwealth Avenue, now named the Louise Holman Fisk House. It had grace and charm. Mrs. Fisk, whom I knew very well, was a dedicated and hardworking woman in the interest of Boston University and its growth and development. When, approximately a year and a half ago, a half-million-dollar gift to the School of Nursing, by a man, was returned, it was the Women's Council which replaced the amount. The sequel is well known to you.

Again, if memory serves me well, Mrs. Larz Anderson, primarily because of her interest in dean T. Lawrence Davis and his work in establishing the College of Practical Arts and Letters for women, tendered the property now possessed by the University in Brookline; and under certain circumstances, I believe that even more land could have been part of this gift undoubtedly enough to have provided a campus for Boston University in its entirety.

The late Alice Stone Blackwell, a trustee of Boston University serving from the early 1920s, was a distinguished human being and an outstanding leader in the cause of civil rights.

Nearly forty years ago, Jennie Loitman Barron, Emma Fall Schofield, and Sadie Lipner Shulman were appointed the first women judges to preside in the courts of the Commonwealth of Massachusetts. Emma Fall Schofield has served for a considerable period as a trustee of the University, and the late Jennie Loitman Barron, not many years ago, was named "Mother of the Year."

You know far better than I about the naming gift to the School of Graduate Dentistry and the relation of Anne Rubenstein to it.

In slightly different vein, may I make another observation. When, about ten years ago, the vice-presidential structure was created, including a vice president for student affairs, the University Council lost in its membership the then dean of women. The contributions of Dean Elsbeth

Melville had consistently been constructive and progressive, sensitively interpreting the needs of students, both male and female. Her absence, in my judgment, has been a distinct loss in the Council. Harold Case asked us to react in writing to this reorganization if we wished to. I did. Ten years later, my feeling has not changed. I do not mean in any way to imply that the male representation in this area of the Council has been anything but satisfactory; however, the absence of Elsbeth Melville has been a loss.

These are my thoughts. I felt constrained to share them with you in a sort of off-the-record manner.

P.S. Would it be presumptuous for me to suggest that in retirement Elsbeth Melville bear the title dean of women, emerita? She held the title of dean of women from 1945 until 1963. The genius of her leadership was clearly apparent in the design for the housing of students in the developing Charles River Campus. I am certain that colleagues who have worked with her over the years would warmly support such an action.

Gladys Hardy made it clear to me that the president would encourage the recruitment of women. Twenty-seven years later, President Silber, on reading the above communication, said that my views on the position of women in the University had been "clearly vindicated."

VI. "The Bombs Bursting in Air"

Aꜰᴛᴇʀ ʙᴜᴛ ᴛʜʀᴇᴇ ʏᴇᴀʀꜱ, during which the relaxed atmosphere that he brought to campus was shattered by bomb scares and other threats to stability, Arland F. Christ-Janer resigned as president. Calvin Lee, dean of the College of Liberal Arts, was named interim president.

Lee was well suited to the task. He combined a sense of understanding of the students' mood with a disciplined approach to ending the violence on campus. By 1970, the bomb threats had become so serious — five in one morning at the College of Business Administration —

that conducting the operation of the University was seriously threatened. Each time a bomb threat was phoned in, the building named was immediately vacated. On Lee's watch, the University Council adopted a new policy. It ruled that when a bomb threat was received, an alarm would be sounded; the timid could leave without prejudice to their class standing, but classes would continue. (Parenthetically, let me say that while we experienced only a few threats at Sargent College, nevertheless the president of the student council and Whitney Powers, a faculty member, met me at 6:00 each morning to search the building for suspicious-looking objects. We found none.) At Lee's request, the United Ministry — chaplains of the Catholic, Protestant, and Jewish faiths — agreed to hold a "community meeting" in Marsh Chapel at noon one day in October, at which Cal Lee would announce the new policy. In the half hour before noon, the chaplains would conduct brief services in their respective traditions.

The chapel was filled. By noon, there was standing room only. The air was blue with fragrant smoke, not from incense, but from marijuana. The Catholic chaplain had conducted the Eucharist sacrament by darting slices of French bread throughout the chapel, and by moving pails of wine (not grape juice) from aisle to aisle. At two minutes of 12:00, Cal arrived. He announced that he had planned to describe the new bomb-threat policy at 12:00. But as he was about to leave his office, a threat was phoned in stating that a bomb set to explode at 12:30 p.m. had been placed in a hard-to-find place in Marsh Chapel, and therefore he would wait until then to speak about the plan. He said that anyone who wished to could leave the Chapel at once. Of the five hundred present, approximately fifty departed, but they were soon replaced by others.

At exactly 12:30, Cal arose from his seat in the front pew to announce the new policy. He told me after the meeting that just before he began to speak, he had glanced at the floor in front of the pulpit. His eyes were caught by a headstone, which read, "Here lie the ashes of Daniel L. Marsh. . . ." In frightened bewilderment, Cal had wondered if his own ashes might soon land on top of the headstone marking President Marsh's grave.

Colleen Morrissey (Sargent College '83), Dean George, and John Silber at the Sesquicentennial Gala. 1989.

The John Silber Era

I.   Which Shall It Be? Which Shall It Be? John Silber or Cal Lee

II.   Inauguration — A Fitting Commencement Event; "The Pollution of Time" — A Timely Address

III.   The Socratic Method and the University Council

IV.   "I Fooled You, George" — My Alumni Award

V.   A Convocation, A Reception: *But* "Yes, We Have No Bananas" or Anything Else

VI.   Retirement: Boredom or Bliss?
      A. In Europe
      B. We Turn Again Home
      C. *Optimal Health: The Quest — A History of Sargent College*

VII.   "Blending Sadness and Gladness in One" — Dean Bernard Kutner's Funeral Service

VIII.   "To Be or Not to Be" — Fifth-Year Assessment of John Silber

IX.   Hidden Humaneness Leads to Pension Increase

X.   Howard Thurman: The Particular Man Becomes The Universal Man

XI.   "How Are Your Spirits Now, Vernon?"

XII.   The Howard Thurman Legacy

XIII.   The Howard Thurman Legacy and the Role of Boston University

XIV.   "To Free the Prisoner"

XV.   Boston University Sesquicentennial, 1839–1989

F O U R

The John Silber Era

I. Which Shall It Be? Which Shall It Be?
John Silber or Cal Lee

Prior to his being named acting president, Cal Lee served on the trustees' presidential search committee. When he became a candidate for that office, he appropriately resigned from the committee and was replaced by senior dean Walter Muelder. Only two months junior to Walter as dean, I became the University Council's spokesman on matters pertaining to the search for a president. The committee narrowed a large list of names to a final few. Hans Estin, chairman of the Board of Trustees, strongly supported Dr. John Knowles, then director of Massachusetts General Hospital. In due course an offer was extended to him. Knowles declined the University's offer, whereupon Cal Lee and John Silber became the new finalists. Ten of the sixteen deans, I included, strongly supported Cal, having been favorably impressed by his performance as president *ad interim*. Candidate Silber conferred with the deans one Sunday afternoon at the Castle. His presentation indicated clearly that he had analyzed the Boston University situation with amazing accuracy, and he presented a plausible plan of action, which would be a general guide if he were to become president. Garbled reports from the University of Texas, however, continued to cast doubts about whether he was the right person for Boston University. The deans supported the candidacy of Cal Lee up to the very moment that the trustees named John Silber. Nevertheless, Silber's clear analysis of University problems and his bold and challenging plans for solutions could not be gainsaid. So with some trepidation, unallayed by the word that Silber was not averse to using the "tremble" factor, the deans received the new president.

When he was officially chosen, I wrote to him saying that as a longtime member of the University family, I extended a welcome; that I would like him to meet with the Sargent faculty and to economize his time suggested that it be at a breakfast meeting; and that as a senior dean I had experienced misgivings about his appointment. I noted that I had been favorably impressed with his statements about his plans for the University. I concluded by saying, "As long as I am dean, you may count on my support." Fortressed by profound respect for him and his accomplishments, that support continues to this day — always agreeing with him on specific matters, of course not. Admiring him for his dedicated commitment and for recognizing the critical needs of the University and facing them head on, I salute him.

In 1926, Marsh found a university in sore need of unification; forty-five years later, Silber found the same institution in dire need of a policy focused on academic excellence and attuned to the genius of Boston University. He would design a program to provide services not emphasized at neighboring Harvard University or the Massachusetts Institute of Technology, while at the same time strengthening the curricular offerings common to all universities.

Recognizing new emphases in health-care provision, he gave welcome support to medicine and the allied health professions. Sensitive to the arts and their contribution to the timbre of society, he gave a new thrust to the University's well-established programs in fine and applied arts.

He faced serious problems head on. While Boston University had been a Mecca for local and regional students, the opening of a branch in Boston of the University of Massachusetts, with a tuition rate approximately one-tenth that of Boston University, posed a serious threat to enrollment. Recognizing this stark reality while still only a candidate for the presidency, Silber told the trustees that Boston University had at most "five years of grace" in which to initiate a pattern for survival.

Silber's alarm echoed discussions with Dean Wilde in the early 1930s. Still in my youth, I was startled to an awareness of such a possible problem when Wilde prophesied, "If the University of Massachusetts ever establishes itself in this city, Boston University is doomed." Dean John Patton Marshall shared Wilde's gloomy prediction.

Fortunately, John Silber recognized the threat and courageously transformed the University to meet and overcome it. His north star was and continues to be "excellence," and in time he developed programs to attract students, both undergraduate and graduate, from all over the nation and the world. In 1992–1993, four thousand international students from 128 different countries enrolled.

Silber also joined the president of the University of Massachusetts, Robert Wood, to form a Committee of Cooperation, the purpose of which was to avoid "duplication of effort." That action was seemly, especially since Boston University had cooperated years before with the University of Massachusetts's parent school, the Massachusetts College of Agriculture, in both providing courses and conferring degrees.

During the five-year period of "grace," Silber introduced programs that laid the foundation for survival. Notable, and perhaps the cornerstone of the new foundation, was the establishment of The University Professors program. He has continued to move the institution to a higher plane of academic excellence and has not neglected the physical environment, creating an ambiance of beauty on the Charles River Campus with well-placed trees, flowers, and fountains.

Silber brought to the University a personal record of scholastic excellence. He was an internationally recognized authority on the philosophy of Immanuel Kant and was a recipient of the Danforth Foundation's E. Harris Harbison Award for Distinguished Teaching. His students in philosophy at the University of Texas responded enthusiastically to his Socratic teaching method. He had been a visiting professor at the University of Bonn in 1959–1960 while on a Fulbright research grant and later was a fellow at King's College at the University of London. Himself a disciplined, hardworking scholar and administrator, he expects no less of his colleagues.

II. Inauguration — A Fitting Commencement Event
"The Pollution of Time" — A Timely Address

THE INAUGURAL CEREMONY for John Silber was a fitting part of the 1971 Commencement. The setting at Nickerson Field made possible an audience of fourteen thousand, including students, alumni, parents, distinguished guests, and friends of Boston University. Silber's address, "The Pollution of Time," ranks among the best, if not the best, in the institution's long history. *The Boston Globe* described it as "an eloquent and auspicious beginning." A veteran television newsman declared it to be "easily the most significant commencement speech I ever heard." Silber was indeed eloquent, and more than that, what he said was substantively significant: "All over the nation we hear cries of alarm about the pollution of air and the pollution of water; but we hear little about a pollution far more serious — that of time itself." And he warned, "But when the structure of time is destroyed, the basis for significance in our own lives is destroyed. All meaning is lost in the instantaneous . . . instant friendship, instant sex, even instant marriage — marriage that can be dissolved immediately after instant consummation." He called for a renewed emphasis upon the study of history, so that the individual may "recapitulate aspects of human history in his intellectual and spiritual development. . . . Education must change in profound ways to meet cultural changes. We must gain the same respect for time that the American Indian had for nature, for time is a part of nature."

III. The Socratic Method and the University Council

HIS WELL-KNOWN propensity for using the Socratic method was at work as Silber presided at a meeting of the University Council in 1971. Stuart Groat, chairman of the University committee on degrees and degree programs, described a program for a doctoral degree submitted by the faculty of the School of Nursing. Speaking on behalf of the committee, he moved that the proposal be approved.

I seconded the motion and said that Sargent College would soon propose a Doctor of Science program in a discipline of the allied health professions. There ensued a Socratic dialogue between Silber and me. His opening challenge, which I paraphrase only slightly, was, "Do you mean that you will be proposing a Ph.D. degree in allied health?!" My reply was that Sargent College would be proposing a Doctor of Science program in a discipline of allied health and that I considered physical therapy nearly ready to conduct such a curriculum. After twenty minutes of bantering back and forth, during which he continued to use the general term "allied health," I noted that the dean of the Graduate School had initiated with the deans of health-related schools a discussion of the merits of a doctoral program in health similar to those in academic fields. The question that the dean raised for such a discussion related to the growing number of health centers and the need for administrative leadership not confined to a specific discipline, such as medicine, nursing, or dentistry.

I recall saying, in effect, "Mr. President, since you persist in talking not about a specific program but about a general one, let me respond to that challenge. Not immediately but in the future, such a general program could meet a real need. In my judgment it could be as meritorious as a comparative degree in philosophy." Silber smiled, the question was called for, and the motion passed unanimously.

When the meeting adjourned, Silber put his arm on my shoulder and said, "You put up a great defense, George."

Too often sensitive people, students, faculty, and others, feel that they are put down in discussions with Silber. More often the opposite is true. "Systematic doubt and questioning" is intended to "elicit a clear expression," or to expose ignorance about a given subject when the discussant is ill-informed. Is not the process of strengthening the individual in thought and its expression a hallmark of an effective educator?

IV. "I Fooled You, George" — My Alumni Award

WITH MY "RETIREMENT" soon to come on August 31, 1972, the General Alumni Association generously included me among nine recipients of the association's award. The ceremony was held in the fall of 1971 at a dinner in the Copley Plaza. John Silber was the after-dinner speaker. He focused his remarks on the recipients, holding me to the last. About the others, his comments were serious and made with presidential dignity. About me — uh oh! "And now we come to Makechnie," he said, and continued, "When I arrived on campus, I found the University's financial situation far worse than it had been painted. I naturally turned to the nearest Scot. Describing the situation to Makechnie, I asked him what he would recommend to get the situation in balance. George said [and here Silber began speaking in a perfect Scottish burr], 'I can't help you with the academic part of the problem, but I can with the dormitories. I find that in my household a diet of oatmeal is most economical, and if we cook enough on Sunday to last the week, we save even the more. On Sunday, the oatmeal tastes verra goud, but by Saturday it's 'orrible. But I says to myself, down it once more and then reward yuself with a glass of Scotch. With me mouth tasting awful from the oatmeal I take a glass, fill it with whiskey, and lift it to me lips. I hold it there for a moment to get the smell of it, and then pour it back into the bottle. When the glass is empty, I say, 'I fooled you, George!'"

Otto Zausmer and his wife, Elizabeth, were guests at the 1972 Alumni Awards ceremony. Otto was an associate editor of *The Boston Globe*. He believed John Silber's kidding, especially that he had turned to me for help with the University's financial problems. The next day, I had a phone call from the *Globe*'s financial editor, who said that Otto had told him that I knew more about the University's financial condition than anyone else. He asked for an interview. Fearing a garbled story in the *Globe*, I saw him in person to give him the facts and to let him know that John Silber has a sense of humor — a trait that few at the *Globe* have yet grasped.

To my surprise and delight, Howard Thurman had come from San Francisco to read the award citation. At a social event following a Howard Thurman convocation fifteen years later, once again John Silber was in a kidding mood. He told the guests that he had not heard Thurman give a lecture or preach a sermon. The only time he had heard him speak he had absolutely nothing to say — he read a citation of an award to George Makechnie; but his style of delivery was such that you knew he could read from a telephone book and it would sound eloquent. Knowing that some of the guests were unaware of the friendly repartee we had enjoyed together, he told the group that I would later get back at him. I did. At an appropriate time, I told another group about the posed photograph of Silber cutting the barber's hair in the shop we both frequent. And I declared that I peek in the window to see which barber is on duty. If it's Silber, I run away!

V. A Convocation, A Reception
But
"Yes, We Have No Bananas" or Anything Else

A UNIVERSITY CONVOCATION honoring my retirement took place in the spring of 1972 in the Law Auditorium. Jean Mayer, then a professor at the Harvard School of Public Health and a member of the professional advisory committee for Sargent College, gave the address. Lewis Rohrbaugh, vice president and director of the Medical Center, presided in lieu of John Silber, who was ill.

The evening before our event, I received a call at home from Staton Curtis, the dean of students. He informed me that the entire George Sherman Union building, in which his office was located, had been "taken over" by rebelling students. He asked if he might use my office at Sargent College, which was just across the road from his. Of course I agreed. Soon after the dean's call, I received another from my assistant, Barbara McMahon, asking if under the confusing circumstances we should cancel the convocation. "No," I replied, "the University must not give in to lawlessness." "But," she reminded me, "Food Service can't provide goodies for the reception." "So what; we didn't serve refreshments at our wedding in 1933 because the Great Depression wouldn't let us. But we were married, and I shall retire." (Or so I thought!)

Before we lined up for the processional, Anne, Jean, and I saw a police officer being placed on a stretcher in an ambulance. He had been hit on the head by a rock. To reach the auditorium, my son-in-law Colin's mother and father walked between lines of police dogs in back of the union building.

In that super-charged atmosphere, we were about to begin when Lew Rohrbaugh approached me. He had just learned that the rebellious students thought that Silber was really faking illness and was with us, and that the students would "invade" the auditorium during our ceremony to confront the president with their demands. Lew asked, "If they come, what should we do?" I said, "When they start coming in, no matter who is speaking, turn the meeting over to me." I told him that I would bid the students welcome and say, "You may also attend the reception in Barrister Hall as my guest; but for reasons you know right well, there will be no food served."

They did not come. Later I learned that instead they aimed their wrath at the Registrar's Office, damaging a computer there.

VI. Retirement: Boredom or Bliss?

HAVING REACHED THE AGE of sixty-five, then the University's age of retirement, on January 6, 1972, I finished my service as dean of Sargent College on August 31 and by action of the president and trustees became "dean emeritus." My successor, Bernard Kutner, a highly regarded member of the staff at Albert Einstein College, had been appointed. With the sense of relief that so many who have been administrators feel when "we lay our burdens down," Anne and I sailed for Europe in September. It was the first opening of the academic year that I had missed in forty-five years.

A. In Europe

I was free also of the responsibilities that had been mine when, in 1953, I gave an address to the British Association of Organizers and Lecturers in Health and Physical Education at Oxford University and wrote the account of the organizing meeting of *L'Association Internationale d' Education Physique pour les Femmes et les Jeunes Filles* in Paris. While there, I had met with members of the school committee for the Paris schools to describe the school camping program at Sargent College. And I was also free of the responsibilities incumbent upon me in a 1963 visit: setting up the Sargent College course (not teaching it) in "proprioceptive-neuro-muscular facilitation" at the Copenhagen County Hospital in Denmark and once again speaking to the British Association of Organizers and Lecturers in Physical Education. Ten years after my first address to that association at Oxford, I gave the "conference address" in 1963 at Lough-borough College in central England.

The "retirement" visit to Europe in 1972 was a lark, visiting for-mer haunts and, even more rewarding, renewing fellowship with col-leagues and friends. When I met him, in 1953, Albert Bilborough was the organizer (we would say "supervisor") for health and physical educa-tion in Lancashire County, the locale of the lakes and rolling hills and dales of England. While we were at Oxford, he had been elected associa-tion president. We remained close friends until his death, and to this day I keep in touch with his widow, Ethel.

It was a joy to have Albert and Ethel with us for a weekend in Lon-don in 1972. Of course, we visited Oxford again, and stories from our 1953 stay there came back to mind, particularly an experience at the conference dinner. That event, with a dance following, came the eve-ning before my morning address. True to British custom, a spokesman for the attendants was appointed to respond to my presentation. Alan Morrison, the respondent, was also chairman of the conference-dinner committee. In preparation for his response, he wanted to become acquainted with Anne and me that evening. Riding with us and the Bilboroughs to the dance, we discussed the dinner. Queen Elizabeth had been crowned only a few weeks before, and the rules of etiquette were being strictly followed. At the dinner, all was hush-hush until the toast to the queen. Anne was attended by the mayor of the city of Oxford and I was the escort for his wife. Seven toasts were given, including one to Anne and me, the "guests from America." The final toast was offered by an elderly man, a man of my present age, the founding president of the association. He went on and on, and on some more! (Not unlike me — there are those of my friends who from time to time remind me that in my old age my natural proclivity for talking hasn't diminished any!) Noticing that the waiters in their spotted black "Prince Alberts" in the rear of Wadham College's Great Hall were getting restless, anx-ious "to get on with it," Morrison quietly urged them to be patient. He said, "Fellows, I know you want to serve the meal and get home, but the man who is speaking is old and has done great things in years gone by, including founding our association. He has lived a long and useful life." Whereupon the chief waiter responded, "Y'Gad, he's reliving every bloody minute of it, isn't he?"

B. We Turn Again Home

After seven enjoyable weeks in Europe, Anne and I returned home in November. Anne resumed her work in real estate and I became consumed by the Watergate scandal. We were both proud of Boston University alumna Barbara Jordan and her effective eloquence on the House committee on impeachment of President Nixon. However, we were distressed by President Ford's complete pardon of Nixon without any confession.

Purposefully, I stayed away from the University during the remainder of the first semester of 1972–1973, to give Bernie Kutner free reign in establishing his priorities and procedures without a hint of influence from me. Soon I learned from my long-time secretary, Barbara McMahon, that my absence was being interpreted by Kutner as an indication of my disapproval of his policies. Visiting him to assure him of my enthusiastic support, I received a challenging assignment: to write a book on the history of Sargent College. The time for such an undertaking was propitious. In 1979, the college would mark its fifty-year membership in Boston University. In 1981, it would celebrate the centennial of its founding. Bernie told me that President Silber supported the idea of my writing the college history. In due course, the president honored the effort by writing the foreword to *Optimal Health: The Quest — A History of Boston University's Sargent College of Allied Health Professions.* We chose that comprehensive title because the college had become a nationally recognized model in the developing movement toward a more synergistic alliance in the health professions.

Above. John and George. 1971.

The new first family at home:
Kathryn and John Silber and their
children. 1971.

Dean George and students in the George K. Makechnie Instructional Resource Center at Sargent College. 1977.

Howard Thurman and John Silber at the dedication of the Howard Thurman Room in Marsh Chapel. 1978.

Professor Elie Wiesel and John Silber. 1977.

Below. At the celebration of Sargent College's fifty-year membership in Boston University and the publication of Optimal Health: The Quest, *(from left) Ethleen Diver; John Silber; Dean George; his granddaughter, Karen; her mother, Judith; her father, Norman Makechnie; and her cousin Bradford Diver. 1979.*

Below. Granddaughter Karen Makechnie referees George and John. 1992.

Above. Boston high school students with Dean George at a Howard Thurman Center weekend program at Sargent Camp. 1990.

Right. President Silber, President and Mrs. Bush, and President and Mrs. Mitterrand at the Boston University Commencement. 1989.

Sue Bailey Thurman signs the deed of gift to Boston University of the Howard Thurman Archive, containing his papers and the original tapes of his lectures, meditations, and sermons; (from left) Howard Gotlieb, director of Special Collections, Mugar Memorial Library; William Harvey, University general counsel; George Makechnie; Edwin Penn, vice president. 1984.

Kathryn Silber, Sue Bailey Thurman, and John Silber at the dedication of the Howard Thurman Listening Room.

C. Optimal Health: The Quest — A History of Sargent College

Writing the college history was a three-year project, with two years in the archives of Sargent College in Mugar Memorial Library, and at Harvard University and its Radcliffe College; in each location, papers of Dudley Allen Sargent are housed. The materials at Harvard and Radcliffe were highly revealing.

Sargent College came into being in 1881, primarily to train personnel in Dudley Allen Sargent's theory and methods. As a member of the Harvard faculty, he was teaching physical training and physiology at the new Institute for the Collegiate Instruction of Women, which was to become Radcliffe College. He needed instructors to help him there and at other institutions where his work was in demand. My research reinforced my understanding of founder Sargent's early intention for the work of his school: to train health experts for health-related institutions and directors of health services for the new colleges for women. When his school had only a one-year curriculum, he required his graduates to earn an M.D. degree in an accredited school of medicine before he would grant them Sargent School's full certificate. Of the school's first forty-eight graduates, eleven qualified for the certificate. They became directors of what today are called "student health services" in young colleges for women, including Bryn Mawr, Mount Holyoke, Oberlin (like Boston University, a pioneer in coeducation), Smith, and Vassar.

At the turn of the century, the phenomenal development of public secondary education created a demand for teachers of physical education. Still clinging to his health-specialist emphasis, Dr. Sargent responded by increasing the curriculum to three years. "The better to carry out the work of the School and make it more serviceable to the community at large," he said, and in 1906 established departments: Normal (teacher education), School Hygiene, Domestic Hygiene, Occupational Hygiene, Recreative, Remedial, Spinal Curvature. Convinced himself that physical training embraced all of these areas, Sargent believed that the departmental organization would help students sense the breadth of the subject. While he accepted some students, clients, and patients for the work of specific departments, he required diploma candidates to take courses in every department. He received patients in the Remedial

Department for treatment of "defects, weaknesses, or deformities that are amendable by physical methods" and clients in the Recreative Department for the acquisition of skills "to attain poise, grace, and suppleness" and "to build up their physiques," that they might "enjoy healthful living." He enrolled "parents and would-be homemakers" in the Department of Domestic Hygiene "to inform them of the properties of food and the requirements of nutrition" and of "the need for good sanitation." More than sixty years before the Congressional Occupational Safety and Health Act of 1971, he opened the Department of Occupational Hygiene to enable his students to "study the effects of arts, trades, and professions upon health and longevity" and deal with "working conditions leading to ill health and physical defects." Through the Spinal Curvature Department, he made an arrangement with Boston Children's Hospital whereby all seniors, on a rotating basis, spent the equivalent of one month in the hospital's orthopedic clinic. Under supervision, the students gave patients prescribed exercises, and they studied cases of spinal curvature and other deformities. The Spinal Curvature Department not only provided valuable clinical experience to students, it also foreshadowed developments in physical therapy. While Sargent continued the work of the Spinal Curvature and other departments until 1918, after 1904, in response to the needs in public education, he increasingly centered the work of the school in the Normal Department. Through the next half century, the Normal Department carried out what became the school's primary function — preparation of teachers for the public schools.

In 1908, Sargent reiterated his conviction that those who entered the physical training program to become directors and practitioners should supplement their technical preparation at the school with liberal and medical education in a college or university. He urged them to acquire a background in biology and botany, "be well-grounded in English, have a reading knowledge of French and German," and "be familiar with social problems." In addition, he recommended medical education to increase their knowledge of human anatomy and physiology as well as to sharpen their skills in physical examination and diagnosis. He counseled those who planned to teach in elementary and secondary schools to acquire "all the technical knowledge of the hygien-ist and some of the scientific attainments of the physician." Sargent implored school officials to employ only supervisors and teachers who had this broad preparation.

Such was his lofty conviction. But public school officials would not, and probably could not, meet it. Nor could his students. When, in 1929, five years after Dudley Sargent's death, the school became a mem-ber of the University, it primarily trained teachers of physical education without the exacting requirements that Sargent had held so dear.

Now in retirement, I reflect often upon my twenty-seven years as dean of Sargent College. Humbly rewarding is the memory of the expe-rience in which, with the sometimes-reluctant but nonetheless coopera-tive assistance of the faculty, we transformed the school back to the founder's original intention. The allied health curricula, with its pro-grams all leading from bachelor's, through master's, to doctoral degrees, fulfill Dudley Allen Sargent's fondest dreams for his school.

In the loft of a barn, euphemistically called a "carriage house" because its principal use was to store horse-drawn carriages, the school began in 1881. Today Sargent College enjoys an attractive building six stories high with appointments designed to serve its special needs and a laboratory in the basement to provide cadaver-dissection facilities for gross anatomy classes. I salute Dean Nancy Talbot for her convincing presentation of the need for such a building. A discerning president, John Silber, and through him the trustees understood that by assisting individuals to attain optimal health, the college also helps society meet three timely needs: to provide improved health care, to reduce the num-ber who require the costly treatment of acute illness, and to lift the handicapped from economic dependence to economic productivity.

I am humbly grateful that not only does the Instructional Resource Center continue to bear my name in its new location but so also does the two-story atrium, with its charming balcony, carry the name Makechnie.

VII. "Blending Sadness and Gladness in One" —
Bernard Kutner's Funeral Service

ON DECEMBER 10, 1975, it became my sad privilege to conduct with Rabbi Joseph Polak, the rabbi of the Boston University community, the funeral service for Bernard Kutner: a privilege in that our friendly relationship was so close that Elizabeth, Bernie's widow, requested that I do it; sad because of the loss of a friend and a highly promising dean of Sargent College. As dean, he had continued the development of the allied health concept, found appropriate space, and completed the task of transferring the programs in rehabilitation counseling and speech pathology and audiology from the School of Education to Sargent College. He had suffered a fatal heart attack on December 9.

As the grave digger scenes in *Hamlet* bring comic relief to the plot, so Sister Madonna Murphy's observation of me wearing a yarmulke did to the funeral. Sister, the assistant vice president for academic affairs at that time, had not yet met me. Joe Polak's particular religious tradition left me alone with the closing half of the service. On Sister's return to her office, she said to Vice President Dean Doner, "I have known Polish rabbis, German rabbis, and others of different national backgrounds, but Makechnie was the first Scottish rabbi to cross my path." Dean laughed. Bernie Kutner, who had a keen sense of humor, would have laughed, too.

VIII. "To Be or Not to Be" —
Fifth-Year Assessment of John Silber

IN AN EARLY CONFERENCE, Silber asked me to support a proposal that he and the deans be assessed at three-year intervals. The deans were then reappointed annually, a process which had become perfunctory. I suggested that while three years might be the right period for deans, it seemed to me to be too brief a period for the president. I told Silber that President Marsh had once told me that he didn't feel that he had "full grip" on things until he had served seven years. Silber felt that in the 1970s everything was moving at so fast a pace that seven years would be too long, even longer than the entire tenure of most university presidents. He settled on a five-year review.

When the fifth anniversary of Silber's tenure came, in January 1976, the trustees formed a committee to evaluate his work. The changes he had felt compelled to make to ensure the University's progress had taken their toll on his relationship with the faculty. Any major change in an institution's procedures evokes resistance by those who felt secure in established patterns. On a lower plane, as dean I experienced resistance and discontent from alumni and faculty in transforming Sargent College from primarily physical education to allied health. Silber received similar disapproval in a big way. On April 2, the University Faculty Senate passed a resolution citing "lack of confidence in the policies and practices of the central administration with respect to budgetary and educational matters."

The review committee invited vice presidents and deans to testify in confidence about their personal feelings about Silber's performance. Hans Estin gave me, as a dean emeritus, such an invitation. Here is what I said:

> You may recall that five years ago I wrote to you on behalf of myself and ten other deans stating that we were troubled by reports from the University of Texas relating to the displeasure there of some faculty members and others about certain administrative actions of John Silber. The deans turned to me because Walter Muelder, the senior dean, had been named to the search committee for the president and, therefore, could not properly represent them.
>
> Since I was so directly involved in a somewhat negative judgment of Silber five years ago, I feel a special sense of obligation and indeed am privileged to respond to the invitation for an appraisal now.
>
> Silber is often labeled as controversial. Other university presidents who have been articulate spokesmen for higher education and who have lifted their own institutions to higher levels of academic excellence have also been so labeled. In the early years of their administrations, such

leaders were vehemently criticized and their policies opposed by faculty colleagues and others.

For example, Charles W. Eliot was named president of Harvard University in 1869. He was a man of vigorous mind and strong convictions. Unhappy with the mood of self-satisfaction and complacency of many members of the Harvard faculty, he undertook a series of reforms and innovations including the upgrading of legal and medical education, the establishment of a graduate school of arts and sciences, and the introduction of the elective curricular system. Opposition to him soon developed. Samuel Eliot Morison, in his *Three Centuries of Harvard,* writes: "There was consternation in the college faculty at the thought of Eliot: the classicists feared him, the scientists despised him; and both groups communicated their feelings in no uncertain terms to the overseers." Nevertheless, Eliot quickly became a spokesman for higher education. Two of his articles in the *Atlantic Monthly* on "the new education," emphasizing the need of more instruction in the natural and social sciences and proposing to sweep away the strictly prescribed curriculum after the freshman year, had profound influence upon higher education in America.

In contrast to the early opposition, Morison points out that on Eliot's retirement after forty years of service, he was generally regarded by faculty members and administrative colleagues as the most distinguished in a long line of presidents of Harvard and that students who had earlier disliked him had come to regard him not only with "veneration, but with genuine affection."

Daniel L. Marsh, who proved a strong president of Boston University, also suffered some faculty disapproval in the early years of his presidency.

If I recall correctly, in the summer of 1934 a petition was circulated by members of the University faculty calling upon the trustees to terminate the presidency of Marsh. He had been in office eight years. On his retirement, after twenty-five years as president, Marsh was generally recognized as the builder of a better Boston University.

John Silber, in the short period of five years, has become nationally recognized for his articulate defining of important issues in higher education. Like Eliot, he has made substantial contributions through such media as the *Atlantic Monthly* and *Center Magazine*. These have provoked thoughtful discussion among educational leaders. Shortly before being named president-elect of Tufts University, Jean Mayer expressed to me his complete support of Silber's stand on the issue of the independent university and its just claim for support as a contributor to the commonwealth. (Quite likely, the president of the University of Massachusetts has a contrasting opinion!)

Silber has increased significantly the academic stature of Boston University by attracting outstanding scholars to the faculty. He has supportively recognized those academic and professional curricula and programs which, unlike its prestigious neighbor institutions, Boston University is especially able to offer.

As the trustees know, alumni giving and grant support have increased since 1971.

Perhaps less known to the University family is Silber's understanding and concern for the financial plight of retirees. He has given them greater security, pressing for the increased pensions which they now receive.

As Marsh was confronted by an unexpected depression, Silber has been faced with an unanticipated recession. In such circumstances the leadership of the president is put to an exacting test. Cuts in budgets become necessary. Inevitably, faculty morale is threatened and criticism of the administration intensifies.

Silber's administration is not devoid of flaws. Whose could be? Some faculty members, administrators, and students have strongly opposed him. In turn, he has sometimes appeared to be impatient with their reluctance to accept his ideas and policies. In my judgment, this is often the result of one of his major strengths — intellectual acumen. But it creates a serious gap between the president on the one hand and some of his deans, faculty members, and students on the other. It is imperative that this gap be bridged — particularly so in a period of retrenchment.

Communication, in all human situations, is requisite to understanding. Many years ago, in his *Source Book of Social Origins,* W. I. Thomas pointed out that social progress requires mutuality of relationship between leader and those led. This is no less true in a university than in any societal institution. The stability and progress of Boston University will be assured only when its president and faculty, without a stifling sense of uniformity, together find ways and means of achieving unity of purpose.

Though I am no longer administratively active, my assessment of John Silber from the vantage point of retirement is, on balance, positive. I believe that he, potentially, has qualities to become a distinguished president.

Seventeen years have passed since I made that assessment of John Silber. During these years on a volunteer basis, I have been full-time at the University to direct the Howard Thurman Center. Today the last sentence in my assessment would read, "John Silber has become a distinguished president." The trustees gave Silber a vote of confidence and he proceeded to lead the University in paths of excellence.

IX. Hidden Humaneness Leads to Pension Increase

THE CELEBRATION of the tenth anniversary of John Silber's term as president was a festive affair. Tributes continued into the late hours. Deeply touched, Silber responded. I recall that he said he was unaccustomed to receiving so many kind words, and he expressed his thanks.

I can attest to the humane qualities of the man, which he tends to keep hidden. An example of these qualities is apparent in his persuading the trustees to subsidize a substantial increase in the pensions of retirees on the original John Hancock plan. Before raising the issue with the trustees, he asked me to investigate the situation but not to reveal that he was behind the inquiry.

I discovered that not only were many retirees suffering financially, but believing the president was unsympathetic to their plight, they were going directly to the trustees for a solution. When I told Silber of my discovery, he observed that there were legal problems that would have to be worked out and that his concern was that retirees get the increase, not who received credit for it. They did get the increase and I hereby give him credit for it.

X. Howard Thurman
The Particular Man Becomes The Universal Man

HOWARD THURMAN the particular man became Howard Thurman the universal man on April 10, 1981. Thousands of people who had been touched not alone by his message, but more by his concern for them personally, were saddened. Participants in the funeral service represented by their presence the universality of his influence. They included: Lerone Bennett, historian and senior editor of *Ebony;* Landrum Bolling, chairman of the Council on Foundations; James E. Cheek, president of Howard University; Daniel A. Collins, business executive and dentist; Samuel DuBois Cook, president of Dillard University; Sister M. Elise, Sisters of the Blessed Sacrament; Rabbi Alvin I. Fine, professor emeritus at San Francisco State University; Rabbi Joseph B. Glaser, executive vice president of the Central Council of American Rabbis; Hugh M. Gloster, president of Morehouse College; Carlton B. Goodlett, physician and president of the National Newspaper Publishing Association; Nathan I. Huggins, professor at Harvard University; Jesse Jackson, educator, minister, and national president of Operation Push; Vernon E. Jordan, executive director of the National Urban League; William Jovanovich, chief executive officer of Harcourt•Brace

•Jovanovich, publishers; George K. Makechnie, dean emeritus and professor emeritus at Boston University Sargent College of Allied Health Professions; Benjamin E. Mays, president of the Atlanta Board of Education, president emeritus, Morehouse College; Rabbi Saul White, Congregation Beth Shalom, San Francisco; and Sam Keen, editor, writer, and lecturer.

Each paid tribute to Thurman, and on tape Howard spoke to us all. He reminded us once again that "the time and place of a man's life on earth are the time and place of his body, but the meaning and significance of his life are as vast and far reaching as his gifts, his times, and the passionate commitment of all his powers can make it." Running through the theme of each tribute was a testimony to Howard's life as it was sensitively attuned to his times and to all time, as it was redemptive, and as Howard Thurman was passionately committed, always speaking to the "deepest needs and aspirations of the human spirit — to the hunger of the heart." Listening in the congregation were representatives of the humble and disinherited.

XI. "How Are Your Spirits Now, Vernon?"

AMONG THE COMMUNITY leaders whose lives have been profoundly influenced by Howard Thurman is Vernon E. Jordan, Jr., president of the National Urban League, 1972–1981, and chairman of president-elect Bill Clinton's transition team, 1992–1993. At the time of Thurman's death, in April 1981, Jordan testified:

> As we grieve at losing Howard's calm presence and profound wisdom, we glory in the memories he left us, the faith he brought us, and the example of integrity he set for us. I know that Howard's healing gifts helped overcome my own illness while recovering from an assassin's bullet. After I got better, Howard said that he and God were greatly relieved because now he could spend more time on someone else. He and I spoke on the telephone every week. I played tapes of his sermons and lectures. I read his inspiring books. Howard

helped me overcome. He was my personal pastor, spiritual guide. Howard Thurman was my friend.

I personally witnessed Thurman's healing effect upon Vernon. In late October 1980, following my wife Anne's death the preceding month, I visited for a week with Howard and Sue in San Francisco. Although ill at the time, Howard nevertheless agreed to go to a hospital to be with his secretary's daughter, who would undergo serious surgery the following morning. Sue had prepared a light supper for Howard and me. We were about to eat when Vernon called from New York. He was still recovering from the assassination attempt. Forgetting about eating, Howard talked to Vernon for a half hour. His final words still ring in my memory: "How are your spirits now, Vernon?"

XII. The Howard Thurman Legacy

W HEN IN 1971 HOWARD THURMAN completed the manuscript for *The Search for Common Ground* he had a long telephone conversation from San Francisco with me. He told me that the book would be different from his previous publications, many of which were collections of his meditations. He said to me what he also stated in his forward to the book, that when he "completed the manuscript, he made the self-discovery that the book was his 'life-long working paper.' "

He had analyzed his own sense of "the paradox of conscious life. . . . On the one hand is the absolute necessity . . . to savor one's personal flavor — to stand over against all the rest of life in contained affirmation. While on the other hand is the necessity to feel oneself as a primary part of all of life, sharing at every level of awareness a dependence upon the same elements in nature, caught up in the ceaseless rhythm of living and dying, with no final immunity against a common fate that finds and holds all living things."

He discovered that "in human society, the experience of community . . . is rooted in life itself because the intuitive human urge for community reflects a characteristic of all life," that "men, all men, belong to each other, and he who shuts himself away diminishes himself, and he who shuts another away from him destroys himself."

He further became convinced that "the individual who seeks community within his/her own spirit, who searches for it in his experiences with the literal facts of the external world, who makes this the formal intent as he/she seeks to bring order out of the chaos of the collective life, is not going against life but will be sustained and supported by life. And for the world of modern man this is crucial. In the conflicts between individual and individual, between group and group, between nation and nation, the loneliness of the seeker for community is sometimes unendurable. The radical tension between good and evil, as man sees it and feels it, does not have the last word about the meaning of life and the nature of existence. There is a spirit in man and in the world working always against the thing that destroys and lays waste. Always one must know that the contradictions of life are not final or ultimate; one must distinguish between failure and a many-sided awareness so that one will not mistake conformity for harmony, uniformity for synthesis. He or she will know that for all people to be alike is the death of life in people, and yet perceive the harmony that transcends diversities and in which diversity finds its richness and significance."

At the time of the ninety-second anniversary of Howard's birth, Rabbi Joseph Glaser wrote to me, testifying, "It is amazing how the influence the man has had in my life grows with each year, instead of diminishing or even remaining flat. I find new meaning in familiar texts, and discover new texts, new not necessarily to my eye but to my heart, to my mind, to my spirit."

XIII. The Howard Thurman Legacy and the Role of Boston University

REFLECTING ON WHAT Howard Thurman, himself, declared to be his "life-long working paper" and his statement of why he accepted the appointment to come to Boston University, Mrs. Thurman and I exchanged thoughts about the role of Boston University in preserving and sharing his legacy. Where should his archive reside? — that was the fundamental consideration. In her home in San Francisco and mine in Lexington, we carried on these discussions over a period of two years.

Other institutions, particularly black institutions in which Howard had been a student and/or faculty member, understandably had pressed claims to him and his archive. But Howard had chosen to come to Boston. He said at Boston University, "I will touch at every step of the way hundreds of young people who themselves will be going to the ends of the earth to take up their responsibilities as members of communities. Conceivably this means the widest possible dissemination of the ideas in which I believe." To be dean of the chapel in a predominantly white university, where the students come from all over the world and are of different cultural, religious, and ethnic backgrounds — such a setting, he mused, might prove to be "a stimulating testing ground for his concept of unity." At the University, and in the Boston community, he might help to build a community strengthened by the diversity of its members.

After this two-year period of thoughtful consideration, Sue Bailey Thurman concluded that her husband's archive belonged at Boston University, where he had ministered for twelve years. In making the presentation, she said in part, "the private papers of Howard Thurman are given to Boston University because he chose to come here after following a dream of unity crossing all lines of race, creed, color, or national origin. This became the motive of his life. This was the motive of his life from the beginning as a young man, as a student, and later as a faculty member of Morehouse College, his alma mater. Then his work carried through this dream at Howard University in Washington, D.C., and then to San Francisco for the co-founding of the Church for the Fellowship of All Peoples; and finally to Boston, to the town-gown community of Boston University. When he arrived here he had learned very many fine lessons which he offered to this community — which, I think, was the ultimate legacy."

Howard Thurman's ultimate legacy! What a rare inheritance for an educational institution. What a sobering challenge to stewardship. How is Boston University responding to the challenge?

Let the president speak first. In 1984, on the occasion of our announcing the formation of an informal Howard Thurman Fellowship at Boston University, President John Silber declared:

> The gospel that Howard Thurman preached was so universal
> that it addresses us all and gives us reason as human beings

to honor his memory and to see to it that this educational institution presents his views to forthcoming generations of our students. The Howard Thurman legacy is a proud part of Boston University, and we shall do whatever we can to be sure that it is not the memory of Howard Thurman that is honored at Boston University, but the *living word* and life of Howard Thurman that become a part of the experience of every student in this institution.

In 1984 we introduced a Howard Thurman Fellowship. When, in December 1985, I proposed the establishment of a Howard Thurman Center to President Silber, his reply was immediate. "Your proposal," he said, "has my full and enthusiastic support." His full and enthusiastic support continues unabated to this day.

The Howard Thurman Center became a reality in February 1986. Its present officers comprise a trustee of the University, the dean of the chapel, the dean of the School of Social Work, the dean of students, the Martin Luther King, Jr., professor of social ethics, the student coordinator of student programs, and Sister Madonna Murphy, C.S.C., special assistant to the archbishop of Boston, Bernard Cardinal Law. Sister Madonna is co-founder of the Fellowship. Sue Bailey Thurman is honorary chairman, John H. Cartwright is chairman, and I am director. The center continues as a unit in the Dean of Students Office, providing experiences to help individuals strengthen themselves as they stay true to their authentic identities and together create a community characterized by harmony in its diversity.

The increasing number of students involved in the work of the center is a most gratifying development. Student members are from various schools, colleges, and organizations in the University. They are of different nationalities and ethnic backgrounds. They are from Christian, Hindu, Jewish, Muslim, and Shinto traditions. They include officers of the all-University student government, but also many others without political portfolios. By any measure, student members of the Howard Thurman Center and its Fellowship constitute a representative cross-section of the highly pluralistic population of fourteen thousand undergraduate students at Boston University.

The spirit of Howard Thurman continues in the life and work of graduates. Deborah Hoffman Backus ('86) motivates physical therapy patients to find a new dream when, by accident or other cause, the dream of walking again has been shattered. She uses Thurman's "As Long as a Man Has a Dream in His Heart" to show they haven't lost the significance of living. Catherine Rowan ('88) declares that Thurman's "sense of wholeness" gives her strength. She initiated the Thurman weekend retreats at Sargent Camp. Mary Crean ('88, '89) states that Howard Thurman "has given me strength not to give up, even when things are grim." Bettyanne MacCormac, president of MacCormac and Associates, Inc., and a rehabilitation health care specialist, eases the essence of Howard Thurman into the treatment process. Jennifer Hull ('90), Dianne Masin ('92), and Douglas Fye ('92) were student officers in the Howard Thurman Center. His legacy continues to influence their lives and work.

To create a community, a community strengthened by the diversity of its pluralistic student/faculty membership at a university campus or anywhere else, is as difficult to achieve as it is crucially imperative for the well-being and, indeed, the integrity of that institution or any democratic society.

The increasing number of overt and insidious incidents occurring on college and university campuses, and in communities throughout the country gives an air of urgency to our effort. Dare we hope that the sense of community that the students in the Howard Thurman Center are striving to create at Boston University may become a model for other institutions? Dare we? Dare we?

XIV. "To Free the Prisoner"

To HELP THE INDIVIDUAL, any individual "bound or free," to strengthen the self and find inner peace and inner freedom is a central tenet of Howard Thurman's universal message. In order to help prisoners find inner strength and freedom, the center has programs in Norfolk State Prison for Men (MCI Norfolk), Framingham State Prison for Women (MCI Norfolk), and the Hillside Pre-release Center in Roxbury. Thurman's books and tapes are available to inmates. University students accompany me to discussion sessions with the prisoners. Prison chaplains arrange the meetings at regular intervals. The programs have been rewarding. Let former inmates Gypsie Brown, Compton Bowman, and Oren Elow testify:

Gypsie (speaking to me before returning to her cell): Howard Thurman's thoughts help me. I must get rid of the hatred in my heart and put love in. That's why I read about love.

Compton: My exposure to the writings and later the tapes of Dr. Howard Thurman came at a time when my back was to the wall, and the trials and tribulations from exposure to the rigors of prison life had me drifting in a Sahara of misunderstanding and self-pity.

Dr. Thurman's profound wisdom and counsel was the oasis from which I could drink from day to day. He brought meaning to my life and a satisfaction of the "Hunger of the Heart," which allowed me the benefit of the explorations of my own "Me-ness."

There is no doubt in my mind that as a result of my sharing his wisdom and understanding, I have been able to define myself in my environment.

Oren: Howard Thurman said, "Keep open the door of thy heart; it matters not how many doors are closed against thee."

We know that in our lives some people, friends and even family members, sometimes will turn their backs on us, shut us out, close the doors of their hearts on us, even stop loving us. But, we will forgive them if we continue to keep the door of our hearts open.

I, myself, have found out that it is through constant cultivation of one's inner self that love develops.

Society, as well as the prisoner, is well served by an influence that restores self-esteem and instills new purpose in the life of an inmate. Most prisoners are one day released. Without self-esteem and constructive purpose, they are likely to become statistics of recidivism.

XV. Boston University Sesquicentennial
1839–1989

A UNIVERSITY'S EXISTENCE depends upon its achieving excellence in the sciences, the arts, and humanities that far transcends the general norm." Thus spoke John Silber at "A Conversazione on the Metaphor for Our Times," part of the 1989 Sesquicentennial Celebration of the University's founding in 1839. From 1971, when he became president, building upon the institution's strengths, he had moved the University to a level of excellence that leaders of the world deemed excellent. The Sesquicentennial Celebration dramatized the University's world-class status.

The celebration began on March 13, 1989, the anniversary of the birthday of William Fairfield Warren, the first president of Boston University, with an exciting musical celebration in the new Tsai Performance Center. The total event was breathtaking. In April, the University conducted a convocation honoring Jordan's King Hussein.

The 1989 University Commencement was unique in the 150 years of this institution and perhaps of any other. The president of the United States, George Bush, and the president of France, François Mitterrand, were the Commencement speakers. Members of the diplomatic corps from both these and other countries were in attendance. What an understatement to declare it was a memorable occasion! Soon after, in Germany, Silber conferred the University's honorary doctoral degree upon Helmut Kohl, chancellor of the Federal Republic of Germany, who addressed the Boston University Commencement at Heidelberg.

The year 1991 was the twentieth of John Silber's presidency. The Sesquicentennial Celebration had already testified to his accomplishments. In 1991 the Commencement program gave further witness to the transformations he had made: Eduard Amvrosiyevich Shevardnadze, former minister of foreign relations for the Soviet Union, was the speaker. In July, his Excellency Toshiki Kaifu, then prime minister of Japan, spoke at a special convocation in his honor. Both Shevardnadze and Kaifu received honorary doctoral degrees.

The Howard Thurman Center was privileged to present a program in celebration of the University's Sesquicentennial on the theme "Community: The Howard Thurman Legacy." Joining me and Norman Johnson, dean of students, were students from the Christian, Hindu, Muslim, Jewish, and Shinto traditions. The Inner Strength Choir provided the music. Marvin Chandler had composed "Unitus," a song of unity sensitive in composition and lilting in tone, for the center's celebration.

"Life is a continuum." Dean George with his youngest grandchild, Ian George Makechnie, in the Makechnie Atrium at Sargent College. 1990.

Reflections

"THE YEARS OF OUR LIFE," says the psalmist, "are three-score and ten, or even by reason of strength fourscore; yet this span is but toil and trouble."

Perhaps even a scripture needs an exception to prove its truth. I am privileged to be such an exception. At the time of this writing, fourscore and six are the "years of my life." They have ebbed and flowed with the vicissitudes of life — from the high tide of gladness to the low tide of sorrow. But they have been and continue to be fulfilling; and to complete the psalm, inevitably "they soon are gone" and "will fly away." With poetic insight, Yeats expressed it:

> *Between extremities*
> *Man runs his course;*
> *A brand, or flaming breath.*
> *Comes to destroy*
> *All those antinomies*
> *Of day and night;*
> *The body calls it death.*
> *The heart remorse,*
> *But if these be right*
> *What is joy?*

What is joy? In reflection, to me joy is the privilege of living life optimally "between extremities," of developing a capacity to deal with disappointment, to cope with sorrow, to acquire the art of "blending gladness and sadness in one," and to sprinkle life generously with the dewdrops of humor.

Sadness when a dear one is no longer physically present, but gladness for the privilege of having had a marital partner of sterling quality for nigh half a century. Sadness when my closest friend can no longer climb the rocks with me for an ocean-side hour of inspiring fellowship, but gladness for the quarter century of special relationship with one who ranked among the great religious and social thinkers of his time and whose legacy contains a message so universal that it speaks to the human condition in all time.

Ah yes, and gratitude for the power of memory, that power that can make real a presence that continues although physical presence did "fly away."

Living the "life abundant" into the sunset years requires, I believe, that one continues to grow in the search for the "good, the beautiful, and the true"; requires a recognition that truth is dynamic, not static—a realized potential perhaps, but always a potential. James Russell Lowell expressed it:

> *New occasions teach new duties,*
> *Time makes ancient good uncouth.*
> *They must upward still and onward*
> *Who would keep abreast of truth.*

Over the years, I have observed that wisdom is not the possession of the elderly alone. Mine has been and happily continues to be the special privilege of sharing experiences with students and graduates of Boston University. If, drawing upon a resource of cumulative experience, I have been their teacher, so, from the perspective of youth, they have been my tutor. When sharing age with youth and youth with age is done in vigorous dialogue, both grow in wisdom.

Frequently I am asked, "How could you stay in the same institution for so many years? Hasn't it been boring?" No, the situation has been dynamic, not static, ever holding to the timeless values defined in its charter, but always adapting them to "new occasions"; growing from a cow-pasture campus to the attractive Charles River Campus, developing from a commuter, streetcar clientele to a student body representing 128 different nations of the world. Excellence, only excellence, could be the magnet that attracts such a group of national and international students and scholars. To have been part of such a creative development for seventy years has been my rare and special privilege.

In my later years, reflection focuses centrally upon people, upon human relationships in ways understood and sometimes not understood. Howard Thurman observed, "our lives are never left to themselves alone. . . . We are surrounded by those men and women [children and youth, I would add] with whom we identify in our moments of depression and despair and in our moments of joy and delight." I have been singularly blessed: by a loving and supportive family, by stimulating colleagues, by students and graduates who, in ways appropriate to their generation, define my sense of the meaning of immortality. Howard Thurman said it: "It is life, itself, that's alive."

Sons Norman and Arthur, and daughter Joan — what a three-fold blessing! And their spouses, Judy, Heather, and Colin. Ah yes, "one generation comes and another passes away" — but life is a continuum as grandchildren Wayne, Karen, Bradford, Ned, Gregor, Brendaen, Lôc, Glenn, and Ian illustrate each so differently and together so magnificently.

Throughout the pages of this memoir, the influence of University associates upon my life becomes clear: Daniel Marsh, Arthur Wilde, Harold Case, John Silber, and numerous colleagues.

Ah, and the students and graduates:

Deborah A. Backus, faculty member, Georgia State Medical College, who in her generation carries the meaning of the holistic approach to health care provision and relates so closely to each of the phases of my life: the Howard Thurman legacy, the physical therapy contribution, the School for the Arts experience, and those personal relations that bind families in one. She has become a beloved "niece."

Susheel Srikonda, an undergraduate student in computer science and philosophy at Boston University who graduated in 1991 and did graduate work in public affairs at Coro, a foundation for leadership. Susheel brought student government into close relationship to the Thurman Center, stating:

> In a world that can often consist of divisive politics and religious beliefs, Howard Thurman's message sounds a note of unity and understanding. The lessons of Howard Thurman are those of a strong sense of individual self combined with a realization of the goals and needs we all share.

Susan Schaffer, Oxford University Scholar 1990, student of law, who in the Thurman ambiance found a new sense of "spirituality."

Makoto Yoshida, '92, an engineer for Motorola Co., Tokyo, who found from his freshman year the Howard Thurman Center to be a home where he could find inner strength, staying true to his own idiom and yet engaging in activities with students of other cultures to share a common humanity.

Deborah, Mokoto, Susan, and Susheel are from Christian, Shinto, Jewish, and Hindu backgrounds respectively. Let these four "for instances" accent the hundreds of student-graduate relations that have enriched my life.

In summary, deep in the recesses of my mind is the recurring sense that "life itself is alive" and that it is indeed a continuum. But an individual's life on the earth is experienced "between extremities," specifically between birth and death, and we are reminded in the Book that each has its "time." Howard Thurman knew this. He wrote:

> Life and death are felt as a single respiration — the ebb and flow of a single tide. Death is not the invasion of an alien principle, it is not an attack upon life by an enemy. Death is not the Grim Reaper, the black-cowled skeleton with blazing eyes, galloping on a white horse. No! Life and death are identical twins. Therefore it is man's privilege and wisdom to make a good death, even as it is to make a good life.
>
> A good death is made up of the same elements as a good life. A good life is what a man does with the details of living if he sees his life as an instrument, a deliberate instrument in the hands of Life, that transcends all boundaries and all horizons. It is this *beyond dimension* that saves the individual life

from being swallowed by the tyranny of present needs, present hungers, and present threats. This is to put distance *within* the experience and to live the quality of the beyond even in the intensity of the present moment. And a good death — what is it? It has the same quality and character as a good life. True, the body may be stripped of all defenses by the ravages of disease; there may remain no surface expression of dignity and self-respect as the organism yields slowly to the pressure of change monitored by death. These are all secondary. The real issue is at another depth entirely. It is the place where Life has long since been yielded to, where the private will has become infused with the Great Will.

Life and death: The ebb and flow of a single tide.

To my children, grandchildren, graduates, and "good friends, all":
CARRY ON!